The
Lion
and the
Queen
I hope to be....

Cindy Gilbert

AuthorHouse™
1663 Liberty Drive
Bloomington, IN 47403
www.authorhouse.com
Phone: 833-262-8899

Scripture quotations marked NKJV are taken from the New King James Version. Copyright
© 1982 by Thomas Nelson, Inc. Used by permission. All rights reserved.

This book is printed on acid-free paper.

ISBN: 978-1-6655-0620-5 (sc)
ISBN: 978-1-6655-0621-2 (hc)
ISBN: 978-1-6655-0619-9 (e)

Library of Congress Control Number: 2020921467

Print information available on the last page.

Published by AuthorHouse 10/30/2020

author HOUSE®

IN LOVING MEMORY OF MY FAMILY THAT HAS COME AND GONE: MAY YOU REST IN HEAVENLY PEACE AND FOR THOSE WHO HAVE NOT BEEN BORN YET, TRUST IN JEHOVAH.

DEDICATION

I dedicate this book about who I am to my mother Grace who has prayed for me since I was a young child and to my celestial mom through Christ, Guadalupe.

Ave Maria

A bright light shines bright

A beauty that will outlive time

Green and Gold overflow

A face that is pure

A hearts love that will overflow

A power that stands behind

By his side for generations to come

She is in his glory

She prays for those in most need

An unchangeable face

A true love from the beginning

Clean untouchable and pure

Poor in the beginning

Being holy and pure to the core

Promised chastity to her Lord

I also dedicate this to my family and friends who have been there for me and have prayed with me or for me in all times of need.

TABLE OF CONTENTS

I am Cindy. My ancestors come from many different places. I have been told that my family is included in the history books in Nicaragua. My mom Grace and my Dad Benji meet in a Nicaraguan prison during a revolution with the Communist country. My mother Grace was a schoolteacher and municipal of the court of Nicaragua, who was recognized by a previous student of hers and let free. My mother was married to the vice president's son who had left the country when the revolution began. In prison, a love affair began with my parents as they began to speak to each other in the four doors that enclosed them together. Through the cell walls, they could hear the yelling and screaming of people as they tried to get to safety. In some ways grateful that they were in prison as outside the prison walls churches and houses were being burned down.

My mother's only hope, to get to safety was one of my Fathers daughters who had access to a helicopter to get them out of Nicaragua. Soon after a journey to the United States began as my Father told my mom Grace about a life of opportunity in the United States. With only five dollars in my mom's pocket and no knowledge of the English language my mother began a new life in her early forties as she began to look for a job in order to raise money to bring all of her children to the United States who were left in Guatemala with her mom and dad my grandparents.

Life Journey

Growing Up in Santa Ana CA in the 1980's, I was born in 1982 in a memorial hospital as a healthy full-term baby.

I drowned in a swimming pool at about age 3 after I was pushed in and by the grace of God came back to life. Every day since then has been more than a blessing to my life.

SOMETIMES PEOPLE IN YOUR LIFE WON'T UNDERSTAND YOUR JOURNEY AND THEY DON'T HAVE TO.

I love my family no matter how crazy we may appear to others. We are unique, loving God-fearing people, who have received Gods mercy, love, and peace time and time again. I am super proud of my family, no matter what punches life throws at us we keep getting right back up. (pow) The power of prayer is magnanimous. I cannot say it enough I love all my family.

We are all related means to me that we all have the same Father Jehovah, even though we may have different parents.

My youngest sister is Rebecca and I recall the first time I saw my sister Rebecca. I was hiding under the kitchen table and I recall I was looking out the glass window in the kitchen when my parents came into the patio and I saw my mom Grace holding my younger sister Rebecca in her arms. My mom was wearing a long pink gown. My dad Benji was by my mom's side and they both brought my sister Rebecca into the home for the first time. I was afraid and curious of what they had in their arms, but I soon fell in love and wanted to carry her, but I was too young to hold her by myself, so my older sister Janice helped me hold her while I was sitting on the couch. Every time Rebecca would cry, I would go near her crib and try to comfort her. My sister Rebecca was born bowlegged and she had to wear a brace to correct her legs and every time her legs would get a little better the brace had to be tightened a little more and my sister Rebecca would cry very loudly. Me and my older sister would come into the room and loosen the brace so she wouldn't be in so much pain and my mother would latter find out and remind us that she needed the brace to be on and tightened in order for her legs to be corrected and she

would retighten the brace. Rebecca grew up and her legs were corrected by the brace. She grew up to be a beautiful light brown, light complected female with big brown eyes like myself.

My older sister Janice also grew up to be a beautiful smart female. She has curly long hair; green eyes, is light complected and a good height like me. When I was a little girl, I would notice that my older sister Janice would not speak but would point at objects when she wanted something to express herself. I was told that the reason she could not speak was because the war in Nicaragua traumatized her when she was a young child. Janice went to a special school to help her speak and when she reached junior high, she was able to finally speak and use her words to express herself in both English and Spanish perfectly. My sister Janice loves mermaids and is very feminine. She has a great sense to make a room look beautiful by decorating a room, home, or space in an aesthetic fashion.

My older brother Kenneth was a bully and would love to fight with me, but it taught me to defend myself and be confident in standing up for myself. My brother would fight with me, but he would not allow other children to bully me or fight with me, so I could always go to him when someone would try to bully me. He was my personal bodyguard as a young child. He grew up to be a tall, sensitive man with curly hair who is now a veteran of the Navy.

When I was a young child, I had a lot of toys that were given to me by my half-sister Dana. I had lots of dolls and barbies. I was told I looked like her and would grow up to look like her. I think I grew up to be a unique creation of God even though on the outside I have some characteristics to my biological family.

Friends...

My friends who helped me rediscover my faith and fall in love with our creator. Friends and family mean the world to me, especially people in my life who have been there through the good, bad and the ugly.

Friends and Family helped lead me towards my DAD.

A few of my accomplishments, while growing up…

With regards to my education, I began school at age six as opposed to age five, since my birthday is the last day of the year, they would not let me enter school. I started school with a rocky start, due to a problem remembering things and was taken aside by a special education teacher to review the alphabet and colors. I was not born delayed, but due to lack of oxygen to the brain after a drowning accident it was difficult for me to learn new things. Regardless of my memory problems I was a determined child who loved education and all my teachers. I soon became a particularly good student and enjoyed learning. If I did not know the answers to a question or how to do something, I would always ask my classmates to help me, which made me very social. I received the President's award in the fifth grade for the person most likely to succeed based on effort. I completed every class on time and was an honor student on several occasions. I am a very smart girl and well-rounded individual.

My mother would tutor me in basic math at home, since she was knowledgeable with her background in education from Nicaragua. I would receive front of the lunch line passes as a reward for my outstanding behavior in school and citizenship when I was in junior high. I was involved in clubs throughout all my schooling. My mother has always been proud of the type of person I am.

I would receive front of the lunch line passes as a reward for my outstanding behavior in school and citizenship when I was in junior high. I was involved in clubs throughout all my schooling. When I was in elementary school I was in P.A.L.S, Girls Scouts, and choir, as well as in the D.A.R.E program. In junior high school, I was an honor student, involved in writing the newspaper, Girl Scouts, Choir, Kayaking program, and other after school programs. In high school, I was involved in the book club, Future Teachers of America, Girls Inc., choir, and other programs. After high school, due to my good grades and extracurricular activities I went straight to a State University of Fullerton and there I was involved in a non-denominational church and in Human Services Student Association and obtained the Leadership award for doing the most community service hours from my graduating class. My mother taught me to always try my best and to be a good, law abiding citizen.

A few of my accomplishments have been being awarded the president's award on my fifth grade graduation for most likely to succeed, obtaining my bachelor's degree, visiting the sick and praying for them, being voted one of the friendliest people in junior high school, since I have been taught to always try my best, for the glory of God, no matter how difficult a situation may get. I have learned that it is not about the outcome, but about the process. I am not perfect for only Abba is perfect, but I try my best as a person, sister, and friend to be good to others and may all the glory go to Abba.

Description of my mother Grace...

My mother Grace, a strict, strong, courageous, hardworking, intellectual woman with entrenched religious values from her childhood of growing up in a religious school. She was affectionate in her way and treated each one of her children differently. My mother showed her affection by cooking for us; cleaning for us, giving us money, buying us things that we needed, speaking good of us to others when we succeeded in school and in our daily lives. My mom would lecture me a lot, for me to stay out of trouble and do good deeds. She has strong religious values and a love for the Virgin Mary who helped perform miracles for her ever since she was a kid from not being punished by her parents for breaking an important emblem to the resurrection of her daughter in a swimming pool. She grew up speaking to priest regularly and can recite many prayers and verses by memory. Throughout the years my relationship with my mom has become stronger and stronger. She has been with me through the most difficult times in my life and I appreciate her for everything she has ever done for me. We have become more open with each other through the years and everything my mother says is right because she gives great advise. She has been my guidance counselor throughout my life by listening to all my dilemmas.

My mother and Father would say...

My mother and Father would say that they are immensely proud of me because despite all obstacles that have been placed in my path I am yet to give up. My parents have influenced me to become the person I am today by teaching me their ancestry; teaching me about (DAD) (God) (I am) (Abba) and guardian angels. I grew up praying every night with my mom prayers such as, "There are four angels on my bed side. John Luke, Mark, and Matthew. My guardian Angel in the middle and the Virgin Mary at the top of my bed. God do not abandon me by night or by day. "I spoke Spanish in the home, so the prayers went: (Juan, Lucas Marcos

Matteo, el angel de mi guardia en medio y la Virgen en mi cavesiera. Dios no me desanparies ni de noch ne de dia.) I also grew up drinking wholly water every night before I went to sleep in order for God to bless me and heal every bone, muscle, tissue in my body and most importantly help save my soul and make me a good girl. I wondered when I was a small child why I would drink wholly water and my mother would tell me you will know when you get older. I somehow feel like it brought me closer to Abba.

What I like the best about my culture...

What I like the best about my culture is that I like the large immediate family I grew up with. My brothers and sisters from oldest to youngest from my mother's side: Juan Carlos Rivera, Carmel Grayson, Christine Grant, Missy Jose, Janice Davids, Kenneth Gilbert, Cindy Gilbert, Rebecca Gilbert and some of their children who I have gotten the chance to see grow.

In my family we celebrate Christian and Catholic holidays. We also celebrate American holidays like Halloween and Independence Day. I like to call myself a sister, so sometimes for Halloween I like to dress up as a nun or we do themed Halloween costumes with my immediate family.

Food is a part of a person's culture and I have many different types of favorite foods, starting with cakes especially homemade carrot cake, and coconut cake. I enjoy going out to eat alone or with a group of people. I enjoy all types of food, such as Mexican, Indian, Salvadorian, Greek, Italian, Chinese etc. I love food. I also enjoy making fresh juices to try to stay healthy.

My family has Catholic roots, and I was baptized on November 2001 as a Christian. I was baptized twice in a pool of water, as I fell away from the church and came back to call myself spiritual and believe in a higher power. I also believe in the tooth fairy for I believe Abba can be anything you need him to be.

Cindy was baptized for the second time...

When I was a child, I would play spontaneous and inventive games. I would make tents in my living room like the Indians did and play inside. I would do scrap books and put pictures in albums. I would play with dolls, doctor and patient and marbles with my older sister Janice. I would play Snoopy on my computer and other computer games. I would play cops and robbers with my brother Kenneth and neighborhood children, which was like tag. I would play hostess with my sister Rebecca and neighborhood children where we would turn crackers into crumbs and serve them to each other as main course meals. I would play that I was at the spa with my sister Rebecca and Janice and paint each other's nails and do makeovers to each other. I would play that I was a teacher with the neighborhood children and teach lessons to each other. I would make perfume out of flowers and leaves by squishing them and putting them in water. I would make cakes out of mud and put them into pots and pans. I would play a lot of creative games with the neighborhood children, as well as my siblings. I used to play sports, such as tetherball, dodge ball, basketball, and softball. I used to ride my bike and rollerblade. I learned how to ride a bike when I was in the fourth grade after trying for the first time. When I was in the fifth grade, I had an opportunity to play softball with my fifth-grade teachers before graduating. As I got older, I became interested in painting and doing arts and crafts.

I enjoy going to live sport events to watch baseball, boxing, basketball, and football. I also enjoy playing sports on occasion and going for walks in nature. I enjoy swimming and hanging out.

I have read the Bible from beginning to end and have learned that:

God's story is

A book with many pages

A story too long to tell.

Has a love enough for many.

Explaining the beginning and continuation.

Through the pages in a book and through the wholly spirit living with –in me I have learned to have courage with my Dad by my side.

FIRST JOURNEY – POEMS

I am nothing without you…

I must know you. Tell me more and start with your name. Oh, all I know is I need to know your name. Oh, no, I need to know your name. Oh, you came to my call. I feel your presence and your power and Oh, boy I cry with joy as I learn your name. Oh, what took me so long to want to know your name? Oh, boy I do not know your name and I am going to turn insane. Oh, Boy what is your name? What is your name? I need to know, or I am sure to turn insane. Oh, no, I do not know your name. Oh, no, I do not know your name. Oh, on bended knee I plea. I need to know your name. Like lightning striking in the dessert, it was a miracle. You touched me, while I was living in a dessert. Oh, I really need to know what your name is, or I am sure to turn insane. May I know your name is real by you answering my prayers Father. May you let me know your name by answering my prayers? Oh, I need to know your name. Oh, I need to know your name, or I am sure to turn insane. May your name rise me up again? May it uplift my spirit and bring me to your glory, or I am sure to turn insane. I lift your name up high. May your name be glorified? May your name be lifted high. Oh, Father, may it glorify. Holy, Holy, Holy, Holy is your name; Holy, Holy, Holy is your name: Holy, Holy, Holy is your name. May it work miracles in our lives; May it work miracles in our lives. Oh, Holly, Holly is your name. I am desperate for you.

I am nothing without you. I must know you. Tell me more and start with your name. Oh, all I know is I need to know your name. Oh, no, I need to know your name. Oh, you came to my call. I feel your presence and your power and Oh, boy I cry with joy as I learn your name. Oh, what took me so long to want to know your name? Oh, boy I do not know your name and I am going to turn insane. Oh, Boy what is your name? What is your name? I need to know, or I am sure to turn insane. Oh, no, I do not know your name. Oh, no, I do not know your name. Oh, on bended knee I plea. I need to know your name. Like lightning striking in the dessert, it was a miracle. You touched me, while I was living in a dessert. Oh, I really need to know what your name is, or I am sure to turn insane. May I know your name is real by you answering my prayer Father? May you let me know your name by answering my prayers? Oh, I need to know your name. Oh, I need to know your name, or I am sure to turn insane. May your name rise me up again.

May it uplift my spirit and bring me to your glory, or I am sure to turn insane. I lift your name up high. May your name be glorified. May your name be lifted high. Oh, Father May it glorify. Holy, Holy, Holy, Holy is your name; Holy, Holy, Holy is your name: Holy, Holy, Holy is your name. May it work miracles in our lives; May it work miracles in our lives. Oh, Holly, Holly is your name. I am desperate for you.

I AM...

You made your name known to me. You gave me grace. You gave me mercy. You show me the sun. You show me the stars. You show me the way. And I want to praise you for it. Halleluiah, halleluiah Glory to you Father

God, my name is "I am" ...Jehovah, Call me Dad. For I am your Dad. I also like to be called God but call me Dad. I am your Dad.

Courage...

DAD, I have the courage to believe that I am worthy of your love and I will put my trust in you.

The LORD is my strength and song, And He has become my salvation;
He is my Dad, and my Fathers Dad and I will praise Him.

Believe…

Believe in our DAD a Supreme Being

Believe in him with all your heart,

Live for the perfect spirit

Feel his essence in prayer

And happiness will find you

Dad, I meet you in person and through the pages of documents about you and discovered a love that is great, a love that only you can give, a love that is tender and sweet. A love that is understanding despite all imperfections. A love that I desire to keep for I saw beyond the pages and saw a magical presence I wish to keep. Dad, you give me peace and make me feel like a brilliant star. I know you love me weather I am tall, short, fat, skinny, pretty, or plain.

DAD you leave me Breathless…

You know every breath I take; you know every step I make; you know what I am going to say…. Before I speak…. You know when I feel weak you know when I have reached my peak. So that is all I am going to say until I have more words to speak.

What's Your Name?

What is my name? Oh, no I do not know your name. I need you. You keep my heart beating, you are my salvation, you keep me alive and I do not know your name. Oh, what is your name? Oh, what is your name? Once you gave me everything and now, I know you are far, for I have lost everything…. Perhaps if I knew your name things would be different. I must know your name. You gave me everything and now I do not even know your name. I seek and you do not answer. Down on bended knee I call upon thee, but oh, no I do not know your name. How can you hear me when I do not know your name? Oh, no, I really need to know your name. Oh, on bended knee I plea. I really need to know your name. Oh, please tell me. I come to thee for your salvation. I need to know your name. Oh, please tell me for your name is salvation. I need to know your name. Oh, what is your name? Oh, what is your name? Oh, no, I need to know your name. I cry in bended knee. I need to know your name!

Dad, you know every breath I take; you know every step I make; you know what I am going to say.... Before I speak.... You know when I feel weak you know when I have reached my peak. So that is all I am going to say until I have more words to speak.

Phenomenon...

Sad, but true phenomenon; if God does not love me no one will.

Speechless...

I am speechless; no words can describe who you are. My entire vocabulary cannot describe how great you are and what you do for me. So, in the simplest terms I want to say thanks for being you, DAD.

Trying to reach Sion...

Tears in Heaven worth fighting for. Crying to get there, but I am not there. Oh, I am almost there, but I do not know where the soft voice speaking to me is. Oh, I hear you and others do not believe me. I am trying to get there because I know you will be there; I want to see you. Anticipation running through my veins and yet I am a little scared.

Open My Eyes...

I am color blind because I do not see you there. I am blind because I cannot see you smile at me. I am blind and ask you to let me see you. Open my eyes and let me see the goodness in you. May I see your light? May I see your smile? May I see beyond what the human eye can see?

DAD...

An invisible spirit; in so many places at once. Observing all our good moments. Knows when we are bad or good. Forgiving us and being our Dad. You forgive everything but forget nothing. Thank you for your mercy.

DAD, you are before my eyes, but I cannot see you. You see me like nobody else does. You know me in the morning and in the afternoon. You know me inside and outside. You know me forward and backwards. You know me and have seen me, since I was young. I came from you and I will return to you whether you like me or love me, I will forever be yours.

It took plenty of days to imagine and on one day he decided to create what he imagined.

On the first day, DAD, made light

On the fourth day he made stars

On the second day he made water

On the fifth day he made birds and animals.

On the third day he made planets,
which one day will have life

On the sixth day he made reptiles.

The seventh day was a blessed day. And on the day, he made people it was a special wonderful day.

Thirsty for Life...

Thirsty for living water

Clean, pure, and long lasting The Fountain of Youth is DAD

Realness...

Ever wonder if God was real, well it is not until you are in his presence that
one questions their own "Realness." I have the courage to believe that with you
everything is possible. I have the courage to believe in believing

I Can Fly...

Life was short, I was once a centipede with many legs and did not know, which way to walk but now
I can fly. Oh, the life of an insect...Oh, nobody cares who you are or what your purpose in life may be. But
oh, now I can fly. Oh, I am so glad I can fly for God has not abandoned me. He has inspired me to be more
than I thought I could be. The life of a centipede was not all I longed to be. I had a lot of legs and crawled
and oh, I was so glad not to be. I am so glad I can fly and God has inspired me to fly up high and kiss the sky
instead of my life in misery as a centipede with many directions, but with God I have one direction and it's
the sky. With God on your side you can fly like a butterfly and not have to live a life of a centipede. Oh, my
True Father has made me beautiful. I wrote, I Can Fly after having a conversation with God about a centipede
I wanted to kill for being in my bedroom and he asked me to ask him for permission before killing anything
even if he does not answer.

We Are Blind

We are blind! We are blind!

The man was blind; they ran away with his pants and he could not tell.

We are blind! The man is blind.

There was a bomb right behind and he could not tell...

We are blind! We are blind! We are blind! Oh, we are blind, can't you tell?

Oh, we are blind, and thank God the Bomb did not explode...call it ADD and thank God the Bomb was disarmed.

Oh! We are blind! We are blind!

We are blind! Call it ADD or call it whatever you want...

We are blind! We are blind!

For I am sure I cannot see what is right in front of me.

Oh, it is hurting me for I have done something wrong...

Oh! We are blind! We are blind!

Let us turn on the light and see who is there...! We are blind! Oh, boy we are blind!

Can't you tell? Oh…

God and thank you for saving me from this dark cloud that was hurting me because I was blind and now, I can see. Oh!

We are blind! We are blind! We are blind! Call it ADD or call it whatever you want... We are blind! We are blind!

For I am sure I cannot see what is right in front of me and thank God the Bomb was disarmed and please always save America. We are blind! We are blind!! We are blind! Oh, we are blind, can't you tell?

Oh, we are blind. Oh, the effects of ADD, can you see.... Oh, how great is our God for the Bomb was disarmed.

I wrote this poem after having a conversation with God about ADD. My goal was to have a career; be educated, get married and bear children. To my dismay I found salvation and was told none of that was needed in the afterlife. Therefore; I live to love God and encourage you to do the same for that is all that is needed in the afterlife, but if you can do all just the same, always adore the one who made you, Our True Father.

Seeking a higher power is a resolution to any problem…

Seeking a higher power is a resolution to any problem because for God nothing is impossible. We are vessels that can only be mended and made to perfection with the power of the Almighty. Now is the time to pray not only because we are living through difficult times, but because we are living in the end of times. A great way to start to have a relationship with our Dad is by learning his name. Here is a poem about how I asked to know Our Dads name.

SECOND JOURNEY – POEMS

Fear...

Oh, once I was afraid, I could not touch, see, or get close, but with time some of my fear has melted away. I want to be afraid to stay on my toes and I want to have love for him to get close. Some things may appear scary, but if we get close all our sorrows will go away.

Dreams

The dreams I set out for myself in childhood have been improved through time. I was striving for something, but as it turned out life has it mysteries and when I hit the center divider my life turned and gave me an unexpected twist that I am looking forward to unravel and explore every day and for the rest of my life for there is a time and a place for everything.

DAD,

You made your name known to me. You gave me grace.

You gave me mercy.

You show me the sun; you show me the stars. You show me the way. And I want to praise you for it. Halleluiah, Halleluiah Glory to you Father, I have the courage to believe that with you everything is possible, I have the courage to believe in believing

Emergency...

Someone, please call for help.

I need all the help I can get. 911, can you hear me.

Oh, someone call the police it is an emergency.

My call is an emergency and I need help. Help, Help, Help.

The police cannot help then I do not know who can... Oh, someone call the police it is an emergency. (Disconnected Call Beep, Beep, Beep) He cannot help.... Oh, Doctor, Doctor, help me find me, help me find me. I want to be me.

Oh, it can be so irritating to be me. Vicodin, codeine; Oh, so tired of being me. Oh, so tired of being me and living a life of pain. Oh, so tired of being me, Oh so tired. I want to kill the pill, I want to kill the pill, Oh, I want to kill the pill, but Doctor help me, help me I am so tired of being me, Oh, so tired of being me. I simply want to be me. I want to be all that I can be. Oh, no, not the doctor, call the priest, call the priest. I have a confession to make. I am so tired of being me. Oh, so, so tired of being me. Oh, so tired of being me. In a moment, in a second...Forever turned into rain and the rain poured. Let it rain and keep on raining. I need all the water to be me. The pain is gone, but now I simply want to be me. Do not compare me to no one else and simply love me for being me. Love me for being me. Transform me and clothes me. Cloth me, cloth me and help me be a better me. Oh, love me, love me, and help me be a better me. There was light at the end of the tunnel... I dialed all the wrong numbers...your number was not in the yellow pages. (Silence) DAD, answered my call. I love you for you are my daughter. Me: I cannot believe I found thee. (Calm state) (Silence)

I felt like I was judge here on earth when I have a nervous breakdown in my attorney's office due to the auto accident I had. This poem was inspired by that moment.

Puzzle...

Putting the pieces of my world together again.

Like in a puzzle, one piece at a time, making sure all the pieces fit.

I am a part of the puzzle and a part of the solution with DAD's help.

Defend us Father; defend us Father,

Defend us from all the hate in the world.

Defend us Father; defend us Father and may one more person become an angel in the sky.

Defend us Father from war; defend us Father from our enemies,

Defend us Father from those who cause us pain,

Defend us Father from harm. Defend us Father; defend us Father,

Defend us Father and may your Angels help lift us up.

Defend us Father and show us your passionate love.

Prayers, Dad, you are the best. Please help me have self-control, for me to make better decisions in life. May your will be done on Earth as it is in Heaven. Amen

THIRD JOURNEY –
REFLECTION & PRAYER

Trying to Contact You Statements – Invoking…

Most Honorable Father, I call you into my life. Dad I send you a wakeup call. "I am" I need you within call. Dad I need you to communicate with me. Dad I cry for you to hear me in good times and in bad times. Dad I am dialing your number, please return my call. Dad, I am making a collect call. Lord I summon you into my life. Celestial Father I ask that you come within reach. Love, I call you to mind. May you always be within reach to take all my local calls. Call Ring, a Ding, Ding Ring, a Ding, Ding.

Do not forget to call because he can do anything, just think, and pray and give him gratitude and soon he will come and be with you for he loves you more than no one else can. Think and pray, Think and Pray and yes you can. Ring, a Ding, Ding (Hello), Lord most powerful Father, I call upon you Dad to be my all. I call upon you to be my superego and help me make better decision in my life. I call upon you to be my friend. I call upon you to forgive me and love me. I call upon you to help me fly like a butterfly and soar like an eagle and jump obstacles like a rabbit. Infinite Spirit of grace and forgiveness, Dad, I call upon your holly name to obtain all my heart's desires. I believe that in your name I will find salvation.

I give you infinite thanks for creating me. May I always feel your warmth and love. May you always help me endure and overcome all the troubles that come my way. Father who is the highest please heal every bone, muscle, and tissue in my body and work miracles in my life. May your love endure. Heavenly Father, I call upon your most precious name "Dad" to be the white dove in my life and to guide me in all my transgressions. May your presence bind all evil eyes and convert them into positive eyes for me. May I see your light shine in my life in a daily basis. May your light uplift my spirit and soul for me to always jump for joy for being alive. May your presence help me be innovative, creative, and open.

Thankful, grateful, and appreciative…

Keep a daily journal for the Lord on what you are personally thankful for and/ or in prayer give God thanks. I have listed some things in my life that may also work for you.

Dad, I am thankful for you giving me a roof over my head. Dad, I am thankful for my daily nourishments. Dad, I am thankful for you saving me on several occasions. Dad, I am thankful to be able to get to know you. Dad, I am thankful for the clothes on my back. Dad, I am thankful for my five senses. Dad, I am thankful for the peace that you give me. Dad, I am thankful for all the chances you give me. Dad, I am thankful for antibiotics. Dad, I am thankful for you giving me the resources to be able to help myself. Dad, I am thankful for you putting people in my life that give me a helping hand. Dad, I am thankful for all the electrical devices I have that make my life easier. Dad, I am thankful for my brothers and sisters. Dad, I am thankful for all the food chains I like to eat at. Dad, I am thankful for my parents. Dad, I am thankful for you giving me intelligence. Dad, I am thankful for you giving me nature and sounds of nature. Dad, I am thankful for you giving me health. Dad, I am thankful for you giving me National Parks to enjoy nature at. Dad, I am thankful for giving me enjoyable music to dance to. Dad, thank you for giving me entertainment, such as movies to spend my spare time watching.

Dad, I am thankful for organic food. Dad, I am thankful for all the books I have that keep me knowledgeable. Dad, I am thankful for you giving me the resources to have good hygiene. Dad, I am thankful for you giving me the comfort of living in an industrial society. Dad, I am thankful for my smile today. Dad, I am thankful for the clean air I breathe.

Dad, I am thankful for being in a calm state. Dad, I am thankful for being confident. Dad, I am thankful for being energetic. Dad, I am thankful for coffee and vitamins. Dad, I am thankful for being smart. Dad, I am thankful for toothpaste. Dad, I am thankful for you staying with me. Dad, I am thankful that you are helping me on my spiritual journey. Dad, I am thankful for being able to find the words to thank you.

Thank you, Heavenly Father for giving me the resources through my immediate family, friends, and peers to be on my feet. Thank you for giving me the opportunity to experience nature and the things of beauty that surround me.

Thank you for giving me a quiet time where my mind and soul feel relaxed and soothed. I am grateful for all that you do for me, Alleluia, Alleluia. Heavenly Father thank you for hearing me. Heavenly Father thank you for being in my life on this day. Thank you for guiding me and giving me health. Thank you, Father, time after time for all that you do for me. Father thank you for giving me faith and allowing me to nourish it every day.

Thank you for your love and may that love be pure and sweet. Thank you for your blessings and for all that you do that is seen by the human eye and in secret. Thank you, Father for being in my life everyday as I wake, go to sleep and in between when I need uplifting. Thank you for all the times you allow me to feel great, relaxed, and calm. Father Almighty, I know you don't always like to give me what my heart desires, so today I come to you to thank you for all the beautiful things that the world has like photography, makeup, models, a variety of colors, clear blue skies, new designs and patterns; animal prints that were created by your unique imagination and creativity. Thanks for the beauty in trees and nature. Thank you for the smile on infants faces. Thank you for the changing seasons. Thank you for all that is beautiful and thank you for the youth that I had. Thanks for the smile I have. Thank you, Father.

God's Love...

God's my Dad and Dad's love is real. Dad's love can start a fire in any rain. Dad's love can sustain a friendship for time indefinite. Dad's love is a magnanimous passion. Dad's love is everlasting. Dad's love is caring and supportive for those in most need. Dad's love holds the sun, stars, and moon in rotation to the Earth. Dad's love is a universal love that may be understood in any language. Dad's love is unconditional to color of skin, height, or type of hair. Dad's love is shown through all the little and great things we ask for and he grants. Dad's love is for everyone under the sun who is willing to believe in him. Dad's love is platonic for he will also be your friend. Dad's love sustains us. Dad's love gives me the energy to wake up in the morning. Dad's love gives me the peace of mind to sleep restlessly. Dad's love makes me want to be born again. Dad's love is life, for where there is love there is life and a continuation of species.

Build Me Up...

I know I am not the only one but love me all the same. Build me up, do not break me down because then I will not be the same. I need you and want you to love me for without you I will not be the same. Build me up, do not break me down because then I will not be the same. Build me up, do not break me down because then I will not be the same. Oh, Father, I know I am not the same. Time has changed and things are not the same. Oh, Time has changed, and things are not the same, but stay with me and build me up for without you I am sure to turn insane. Oh, build me up. Oh, build me up and love me all the same. I cannot do it on my own. Oh, I know I am not the same, but may your love for me still be the same....Oh Father, love me all the same.........Oh, may your love be limitlessness......Oh, build me up and love me endlessly........Oh, I depend on you to be better than the same. Oh, build me up and love me endlessly before I turn bitter and insane. Oh, be with me and love me endlessly. Oh, Father I want to live with you...I love you and need you.

Strength...

DAD is my moral force. When I am feeling down and broken, Dad is the force that binds my soul. He is the light that embraces my spirit; with him I always feel together. He is the only one who can mend my broken vessel.

United We Stand, we are one... We are tight.... We bind like glue.... And we can do anything we set our minds to do... For we have the power.... We have the strength, and his name means everything... (Jehovah) The fervor that lights my day. With Him, everything is possible.

Strength, DAD is my strength. The salt and spice in my life. He is the delight in my fear. The light in my path. The whisper in my ear. The one that can make me cheer. My family; My friend my all. The one whom created it all. And with him I can do it all

Forgiveness...

Father, Jehovah, have mercy on us. Lord, have mercy on us. God, Father of Heaven have mercy on us. Father of all have mercy on us. God, the Holy Spirit have mercy on us. Our True Father have mercy on us. Father, Son, and the Holly Spirit have mercy on us. Father Jehovah, whose name is holly have mercy on us. Lord Jehovah, most precious have mercy on us. Most wonderful Father, Jehovah, have mercy on us. Heavenly Father, Jehovah, spirit of truth who has mercy on us. Heavenly Father, Jehovah, of love who has mercy on us. Father, Jehovah, of greatness continue to have mercy on us.

Jehovah, master of the universe, continue to have mercy on us. Most talented Father have mercy on us. Most gifted Father, Jehovah, continue to have mercy on us. Most amiable Father, Jehovah, have mercy on us. Most elevated Father, Jehovah, continue to show us your mercy. Great hearted Father, Jehovah, have mercy on us. Magnanimous Lord have mercy on us. Lord who we glorify have mercy on us. Most worthy Father, Jehovah, continue to have mercy on us. Most uplifting Father, Jehovah, have mercy on us. Majestic Father, Jehovah, have mercy on us. Marvelous Father, Jehovah, continue to show us mercy. Miraculous Father, Jehovah, have mercy on us. Amazing Father, Jehovah, have mercy on us. Astonishing Father, Jehovah, have mercy on us. Extraordinary Father, Jehovah, have mercy on us. Father, Jehovah, creator of all have mercy on us. Heavenly Father, Jehovah, whose voice can be the sound of classical music have mercy on us. Lord of passion and all beautiful things have mercy on us. Father Jehovah who installs hope have mercy on us. Father of forgiveness have mercy on us. Most admired Father, Jehovah, have mercy on us. Most wonderful Father, Jehovah, continue to show us mercy. Most loving Father show us mercy. Forgive us for our sins and do not forget your children. Heavenly Father, Jehovah, I am sorry if I have offended you, I beg you to please forgive me and always be in my life. May you forgive me and help me transform my mind and soul because I dread living a life of no hope for the days of tomorrow.

Please forgive us in the same way that we forgive others and lead us away from temptation. Please forgive me with your gigantic kind soul. Most powerful Father, Jehovah, please forgive me for being disobedient, careless and for doing anything that may offend you. Heavenly Father, Jehovah, thank you for being in my life. Thank you for forgiving me daily. Thank you for being with me every day of my life. Thank you for giving me the privilege to get to know you in a more personal level. "I am" have mercy on us.

Confessions...

I confess myself to you and pray that you may renew me for my future actions not to offend you. I confess myself for any times I may have been unfaithful to you, willingly or absentmindedly. I confess myself to you Father for anytime I may have used your name in vein. I confess myself to you Father for any occasion that I have not been respectful to my parents. I confess myself to you Father for any time I have not been respectful to nature. I confess myself to you Father for any time that I have not been respectful to my peers. I confess myself to you Father for any acts that I have done that were impure in your eyes. I confess myself to you Father for any small lies, white lies, or major lies that I have told. I confess myself to you Father for any impure thoughts that I may have had towards anybody. I confess to you Father for any moments in which I have desired my friend's belongings. I confess to you Father for any times in which I have had little faith. I confess to you Father for any times I have not been grateful. I confess to you Father for any times I have not been giving to the less needy. I confess to you Father all the acts that I have done carelessly and without striving towards perfection. I confess to you Father for all the thoughts I have that offend you.

I Hope Statements...

I hope to be rescued. I hope to be able to save money for a rainy day. I hope to be successful at something that I do. I hope to improve my skills and abilities. I hope to have peace. I hope to be happy. I hope to make a positive difference in the world. I hope to make people proud to know me. I hope to change the mistakes I have made. I hope to fully recover. I hope to be happy. I hope to never be depressed. I hope to never be homeless. I hope to make a positive difference in the world. I hope to enjoy my life. I hope for my situation to get better. I hope to make good friends who will make a positive difference in my life. I hope to have things of value. I hope for my mother to have good health. I hope to be a healthy weight and be overall healthy. I hope to always have good eyesight. I hope to be able to make friends. I hope to be inspired. I hope to be creative. I hope to make more money. I hope to be able to help myself. I hope for things in my life to get better soon. I hope to be in good terms with our creator. I hope to be a blessing to the less fortunate. I hope **(your hopes and intentions)** _____.

Hear Our Prayers Father...

Hear Our Prayers, most grand Father hear our prayers. Most delightful Father hear our prayers. Jehovah, the light in our lives hear our prayers. Jehovah, most powerful hear our prayers. Jehovah, who can make our dreams come true hear our prayers. Lord, Jehovah, who can build us up hear our prayers. True Father hear our prayers. Father who enlightens our spirit hear our prayers. Father who is mysterious hear our prayers. Father, Jehovah, who is fresh air in our lives hear our prayers. Father who has the power to send me to hell hear my prayers. Father Jehovah whose love may provide us a fairytale existence in Heaven hear our prayers. Father, Jehovah, of devotion hear my prayers. Father of all hear my prayers. True Father, Jehovah, whose light livens the soul hear my prayers. Eternal Father, Jehovah, hear my prayers.

Prayers to Our Dad...

Prayer is the greatest power that our True Father gave us, and we should use it wisely. I pray for my parents and siblings to always have happiness. I ask for this or something better for them and myself. Oh, Heavenly Father, Jehovah, who can make our dreams come true. Please hear our prayers and forgive me for I am in great need. I am sorry for having offended you and may my future actions in my life help me redeem myself to you. Help me find you and find happiness. Abba, Jehovah, who makes all our dreams come true. Please hear our prayers. Let me feel your warmth. Give me happiness and let me endure and overcome all the troubles that come my way. You who are the highest please heal every bone, muscle, and tissue in our bodies.

Precious Father, Jehovah, who has made his name known to me and who is everlasting. I pray for you not to let me go. Heavenly Father I pray for (**name of the person**) _____ that he/she may have an eternal life filled with love and happiness and that you may grant the wishes of the heart. May you help us find your glory and may you always give us our daily bread. Above all things I pray that your will be done on Earth as it is in Heaven.

I pray for, (**name of the person**) _____, that you may love him/her and give her health. Please put a smile on her/his face. Please guide her/him and give her salt for you are salt. Forgive and continue to love all your children. Heavenly Father, please grant me my hearts desires that are for good. Jehovah, you are my salvation and I never want to lose you.

May you love (**name of the person**) _____ now and until forever. Help me find you time and time again. May your light touch my existence, time after time and may your strength not hurt me. May your love uplift my spirit, and may you always return to me even when times are rough. I understand if you do not want to answer my prayers or speak to me. I acknowledge that I have fallen short in your glory. I also acknowledge that I must brush up on my listening skills and learn to pay attention to your nonverbal cues. I hope that soon you can forgive me and speak lovely words to me. I hope that with each passing day I can learn more and more about you to learn how to please and make you happy. I pray that you are always joyous with me.

Father, Jehovah, whose name has the greatest honor. I pray for (**name of the person**) _____ and that you may always be loveable, kind, and understanding with her/him. I ask that you give her/him everlasting life filled with happiness. I also ask that you may grant them all of the positive desires of her/his heart and that there may be two heavens in order for more people to experience an everlasting life immediately after passing and not have to wait until the end of days to experience heaven or have to wait in the valley of death sleeping until the end of days.

May you lead us away from all temptations and may your will be done on Earth as it is in Heaven. Dad who is among us, I pray that I make positive decisions this morning, evening, night and for the rest of my life. I am grateful for you in my life and pray that none of my decisions cause you to dislike me and for you to put me back on track when I get off course. I pray for my siblings, _____ that they may have happiness. Help us always be healthy and most importantly to continue growing spiritually. I pray that I may always be guided by your holly spirit. May my eyes be opened to my disobedience to you for me to always walk in agreement with you. I also pray that you grant me peace and happiness.

Dear True Dad...

I do not know what direction to take in life. I am poor and miserable. Please give me guidance on what I can do to improve my life. I am in great need. Please open doors for me and my immediate family members. Help me accomplish my full potential in life and in the afterlife. Help me always find the proper usage of words when addressing myself to you my honor. Help ask for this or something better.

May your will be done on Earth as it is in Heaven. Heavenly Father, Jehovah, thank you for being with me. Please help my sister and brother, _____ Father. Please help them have a steady employment. Please forgive her/him for anything that she/he has done that may have offended you. Please give her/him health happiness and a better tomorrow. Please be nice to her/him Father. I ask for this or something better.

Heavenly Father, Jehovah, I pray for _____ Heavenly Father. Please help me help her/him Heavenly Father. Please give her/him wisdom and salt Heavenly Father. Please allow her to be happy Heavenly Father.

Please help **(name of the person)** _____see you and experience your glory. Please help her/him continue with her/his faith. Please love **(name of the person)** _____. Please be kind to **(name of the person)** _____. Please be loving towards **(name of the person)** _____. Please be understanding with **(name of the person)** _____.

Thank you, Father, for listening to me because I know it can be a difficult task to do at times. Help us always have hope. Light a candle and hope to God that you get the things you desire in life. I hope for a better tomorrow. I hope to be worth more. I hope to have more value. I hope to always have health. I hope to regain my strength. I hope to be energetic and alert. I hope to get a career. I hope to be treated with respect by others. I hope to always be self-sufficient. I hope for my family to be able to improve themselves. I hope for greater tomorrows.

Fourth Journey – Test of Faith

Jehovah as I know him...

When I was approximately four, a little boy pushed me in a pool, and I drowned. I recall my soul flouting on top of my body and as my soul was rising, I could look down and see my body flouting in the water. In almost no time God took me to a holding place where the souls of the deceased go. I arrived at this place almost immediately after I drowned and there were other people there. I recall they spoke to me in order to calm me down as I started to cry because I did not know where I was at and the most obvious reason to cry was that I had just departed from my body. The people that were at this holding place were very friendly to me and I thought they were related to me. I recall I stood still, as they asked me to enter the light. My body froze and I did not know how I was going to enter. He then asked me again to enter the light and this time the light became big. I was about to enter the light, but before I did, I asked him if I could see his face first. I recall as I tried to see his face an image began to grow very tall, and then shrink, but he would not show me his face.

I was then taken to a bakery where I use to go with my parents all the time. I soon left the holding place that looked like a cave and arrived at a bakery. I am not sure how long I was at the bakery, but soon after I awoke. I was awakened and brought back to my terrestrial body after being given CPR. When I awoke the first image, I saw was my birth male parent Dr. Benji and I told him that God told me that I would see him again. Today I call Dr. Benji my male parent because my true Dad, which is God told me not to call him Dad because he is very jealous and does not like the amount of people who called Dr. Benji Dad. When I woke up after drowning, I could not believe I saw Dr. Benji. I was then taken to the emergency room, where they pumped my stomach from all the water I had swallowed in the pool and examined me. I remember telling him what happened to me, as well as about the bakery. He was incredibly happy to see me alive and that I did not have any brain damage. He also told me that I had a story I could share with others for the rest of my life.

Sometime after my male biological parent Dr. Benji died. I went to his funeral and it was like a concert because he was loved by so many people it looked like I was at a concert. When I drowned and was in a cave, I was told I would see him again, therefore I always believed that I would see him again in Heaven after he died. I am waiting to see Dr. Benji again in Heaven, since God has revealed himself to me and told me he likes him a lot and that he is in Heaven. During the time my soul left my body my mother Grace had been told by an old lady who appeared at our house that I had drowned in a pool. My mother got down on her knees and started praying. She prayed to Our True Father and our Mother Mary to intercede on her behalf to bring me back to life. A miracle was performed as my soul entered my body again. The CPR I was given along with Grace's prayer convinced Our True Father to bring me back to my terrestrial body. I was resuscitated by the grace of Our True Father. I was given a second chance at life, since at that moment it was determined that I was not going to enter Gods Kingdom, since my body froze as I tried to enter the light.

A lot of time has passed, since then. I had been asked several times if God was real or if I believed in God and if I knew Gods name. I know that I had drowned, but I still could not tell people what Gods name was, what religion to pick or what his favorite color is which now I know is white or what he likes to eat, which now I know he can't do or what defines him, which now I know is love. I would become frustrated with people when they would try to convince me that God was not real. I recall conversations people having in front of me regarding Noah's Arc and if I believed that happened. I recall defending the event stating that drowning is not that bad. When a person drowns, they immediately die. There were many times when I thought the incident that happened to me when I was little was a dream. I have spoken to intellectuals who have great responses and theories as to why the God of the Bible was not real. They have great theories and arguments that have made me very frustrated. I always believed that one would find themselves with God when they died and had no explanation as to why or how God chooses to hear our prayers. I have come to know the God of the Bible more than most and can now say that I know him by name. I believe that a lot of time has passed since the Old Testament and that he has changed some since then. I hope to continue to get to know him and that our friendship may become stronger.

There are many details that have occurred in my life, since the first event to the revelation of God's name......I was baptized Christian in a swimming pool when I was eighteen...I obtained my Bachelor's degree in Human Services with an emphasis in Mental Health ....I have played many roles in life, as a student, sister, volunteer and aunt....I have had a lot of life lessons that have shaped and molded me and I am still being molded and changed by life. Soon after I graduated from college I was injured because of an accident during the summer. It was a sunny day that I was driving to work as I normally did each day. I was looking forward to getting to work because I knew I was expecting a fun filled day with joy as the children I worked with laughed during water play. I looked forward to doing conflict resolution with the children when they could not decide who was out during a game of dodge ball and looked forward to smiling when I noticed progress in children's social skills. Unfortunately, towards the end of the summer of July I was involved in auto accident, which caused me to suffer from a concussion. I was soon diagnosed with post concussive syndrome, which impacted the direction of my life. The migraine's I was receiving from the concussion was one of the main reasons the direction of my life has changed so drastically. Little did I know at the time that an auto accident could cause so much damage to a person. Now it all makes sense, a look of concern and anguish even comes to mind when someone I encounter tells me they were in an accident. I was "teed" that summer and spun out of control several times in both directions. I blacked out and came back into consciousness for what seemed like an eternity, even though it might have been just several seconds. That day I was like a shocked deer caught in the middle of the road by the headlights of an oncoming car. After the accident I was in shock, I felt dazed and confused for several years later.

For several years after the accident I felt very dazed and confused staring into space sometimes for several hours as time passes me by. The medications I took helped this from not occurring that often, but once a healthy female that took no medications was nonexistent. Something very strange happened to me that day, something very spooky. It brings tears down my face to think that at one instant I could be a confident college graduate with millions of hopes for the future and one hit that spun me out of control into a state of turbulence left me uneasy. Thoughts of never recovering came to mind. The voices in my head said, "Oh my, I am a young female who is suffering and in pain and I will always be this way, I will NEVER recover." I had lost hope as I felt I was getting worse each day after the accident. I have learned, since then that we must always think positively, and things will get better. Each day was different, but slowly one could tell that I was no longer the same confident, happy Cindy that everyone had known. There were days where I would lie in the bathtub with ice, to recuperate. At the time I was living with my husband who after having my concussion lead to a domino effect of things which contributed to us getting a divorce, and I could recall him becoming upset with me because when he left to work he would leave me lying in bed staring into space and when he came back I had not moved, I was doing the exact same thing. I was a deer caught in the headlights......my mind was in shock. My mind was in denial that I was injured; therefore, I was still attempting to go to my part time job a few weeks after the accident. My supervisor was well aware that I had been in an auto accident so she was accommodating to me: by giving me permission to not fulfill my responsibilities as a worker; therefore I did not have to sweep or pick up anything for that matter, all I had to do was observe the children. When not being supervised, I would place ice packs on my head neck and back to be there. I did not want to let them know how bad I really felt.

Days went by and the children started complaining that I no longer played dodge ball with them; do any of the water activities, play football, soccer, or any of the activities that I so often participated in. Children were playing rough in the playground and I did not respond as fast as I would have, since I was doing my observation of them from a faraway bench, due to the fact that I was in so much pain. My tutoring capabilities were also questioned when they had never been questioned before. The pain somehow took away my ability to help children with simple math skills. I was then given permission from my supervisor to take time off from work until I got better.

During this same time, my home life was also suffering. My husband who was once so willing to spend all his time with me all of a sudden did not skip a heartbeat to go out on the weekends without me when we were always attached by the hip, while I was left at home in bed medicated with several sleeping/ pain killers. I suppose it was fair, an injured person is no fun to be around with. My friends who are no longer my friends noticed how gravely injured I was, while driving as a passenger with them. My body ached and hurt badly with any little movement and they noticed. It was a previous coworker who referred me to an attorney. I soon scheduled an appointment with an attorney. I went into his office literally not being able to sleep for three months, due to the back of my head and neck being swollen and the pain I had on other parts of my body. I associate everything that has happened to me with the head trauma I received in July. I went into my attorney's office restless from not sleeping to represent my case. I was hesitant at the time to obtain a lawyer because I was under the misconception that some lawyers were liars and cheaters, but I knew that I had to get one by the feedback I was getting from several people in my life that I needed an attorney, as well as the continuation of pain I was having. Having to go see a lawyer, due to an auto accident reminded me of death. Death came to mind because of important people in my life whom I associated with lawyers.

One important person I associated with going to visit this attorney was my uncle, who had once been a lawyer in his country and had passed away; also a deceased friend who never had the opportunity to pursue his dream of becoming a lawyer due to an early death and most importantly I associated the auto accident in July with my death and with the death of my biological male parent Dr. Benji, whom passed away on the month of September, due to an auto accident in the freeway. Death was also on my mind because on the day of my accident I recall a short prayer in my head stating, "God, please help me, I do not want to die." I thought I was going to die and be judged by God. The knowledge that I have of the bible made me feel that I was not prepared to die or be judged by God because I had fallen away from the church. Most importantly I associated my visit with this attorney with being judged by God, due to statements in the bible like one should obey all laws of the nation in which one lives and in my mind I associate lawyers, and political leaders with discipline and judgment.

When I left my attorney's office I felt okay, I went home and felt a little uneasy about having meet with him, soon after I started experiencing awfully bad feelings. I became paranoid, anxious, and nervous. My husband at the time associated this with my lack of sleep. I then felt like I blacked out at the attorney's office and I was getting flashbacks of a traumatizing experience. I did not know where my thoughts were coming from, but I felt that my attorney had put something in my cup filled with water.

Memories of me losing control of my emotions came to mind. I had paranoid feelings that my attorney had put a truth serum in my water that caused me to tell him every traumatizing event that had ever happened to me in my life. I recall flashbacks of my attorney becoming several characters, including God and I was being judged because he was in high authority. I recall me being in the dark, videotaped while saying obscene things. I recall seeing a red light from the video camera taping me, while I was down on my knees praying and asking God for forgiveness and to help me. I blacked out and did not remember for the next couple of years, but a spirit appeared and told me they were punishing me for something I did badly, but for the next couple of years I blacked out and did not remember anything. God did appear at the attorney's office and the attorney tried to defend me, God made me forget what happened and I did not remember until I had felt the wholly spirit years later. My psychosis did not end at my attorney's office, from there on after everything that occurred to me was because of him. I felt that he had somehow predicted what was going to happen to me before it even occurred.

It took me about a year to convince myself that everything that was happening in my surroundings was not due to my attorney and he had not predicted any events of my life in the short encounter we had. I kept telling myself that there was no way he could have foreseen my future in one encounter. Eventually, so much time went on I finally believed he had nothing to do with my life. Whenever I spoke to anyone about my attorney, I concluded that people thought I was crazy. My stomach would hurl when I thought about what happened or what I believed happen that day. I recall memories of me screaming out loud calling for the cops, being videotaped, being hypnotized, overall me having a nervous breakdown because of all the physical and mental pain I was going through in my life, which were caused by that moment. Soon after I left the attorneys office, I spoke to my husband about what I thought happened or what really happened at my attorney's office and he stared at me blankly. The next time I was in the presence of my attorney was to denounce him as my lawyer and pick up my paperwork. I was then convinced that something really did happen in his office as I recall all the lights being turned off and me screaming on my knees for God to help me. The incident that really convinced me was when I saw how his hands were shaking as he gave me my file back. I recall being extremely upset when I felt that my husband did not believe what I was saying regarding something very strange with my encounter with my attorney.

Now I think back and reflect that it is most likely possible that my husband did not believe me because the story I said was simply unbelievable to believe. I suddenly became very afraid of lawyers or high authority figures. I was reluctant to go to the hospital because I had no medical insurance, but the dreadful pain in my head and neck became more unbearable. I could not handle throwing up anymore, having an upset stomach and not being able to sleep. I was accompanied to a hospital by my husband in the middle of the night. My complaints of head pain and bizarre stories, such as the one I was stating of my attorney lead to a CAT scan with a diagnosis of post concussive syndrome. I recalled a male nurse telling me, "by the way, your acting like you'd think you had a brain tumor." I asked him to tell me this in front of my husband, but the male nurse did not. I needed him to tell me in front of my husband in order to confirm to me, what the male nurse was actually stating because at the time I was uncertain if things were real or not and if I was hearing things. I was disoriented and, in a daze, and was unsure of what was real or not especially after what I recall happened with my attorney.

After I left the hospital, my paranoia continued. I somehow thought I had a brain tumor; my brain could not process a joke or exaggeration. At the time a brain tumor felt like it was a lot worse than having a post concussive syndrome, due to the fact that before my diagnosis I had never heard of a condition called post concussive syndrome, but I had heard that a tumor can kill a person. I can recall having paranoid thoughts toward the medications given to me, due to the fact that some of the brand names on them had a "Lilly" seal on them, which caused me to believe that my friend Denice had something to do with my accident, which I find comical now. In my delusion and paranoia, I thought she was in on the sarcastic joke life was giving me, which was the traumatic accident that occurred in July. I also had paranoid thoughts that my friend who had referred me to my attorney was somehow involved in me being in an accident, since she referred me to my attorney and I was determined he put something in my water to make me go crazy which, I find comical now. In my delusion and paranoia, I thought she was in on the sarcastic joke life was giving me, which was the traumatic accident that occurred in July. I also had paranoid thoughts that my friend who had referred me to my attorney was somehow involved in me being in an accident, since she referred me to my attorney and I was determined he put something in my water to make me go crazy.

On another occasion, I believe having pain caused me to attempt to kill myself by jumping over at a beach pier. In my psychosis I became disoriented, while trying to attempt to visit my attorney. I no longer wanted him to be my lawyer, due to the memories I recollected occurred at his office, therefore while driving there I got lost and had an anxiety attack. I called my husband on the phone almost in tears as I tried to get to my destination. Then I recall driving toward familiar sceneries and driving in circles. I started to panic not knowing where I was and somehow ended up at a beach. I parked my car in an empty space, while speaking to my husband. My husband tried to calm me down as he heard anxiety and stress in my voice and confirmed to me that he would come and get me and ordered me to stay where I was. When I got off the phone with my husband without contemplating an attempt to kill myself, I got out of my vehicle and hysterically started screaming and heading towards the pier, holding my head as it throbbed. I was at the end of the pier, while I looked over the pier at the water and contemplated jumping. I was about to put my leg over the pier when someone called me. I suppose someone had called the cops because soon I was escorted into an ambulance and was headed towards a hospital. I recall screaming at the cops because soon I was escorted into an ambulance and was headed towards the hospital. I recall screaming and yelling hysterically in pain and anguish and called for my husband to rescue me like he did the day of the accident. I concluded that pain could make a person go crazy.

In history people had been placed in mental institutions, due to having a tooth ache and now I knew why, since I was being referred to a partial program, due to pain and my suicidal attempt at the pier. I went to a program, were I learned that there were clients like myself who were extremely educated and smart and were experiencing mental problems like myself. During this time, I noticed I heard the honk and arrival of the van that would pick me up at my address before they showed up. I also experienced stress because I was picked up in a vehicle, which also transported people with suicidal thoughts, thoughts of wanting to kill others, wanting to start fires, and who knows what other problems. I did not want to upset the wrong person and be caught in flames for it.

While at the program, I was annoyed while I was attending several groups because I felt that I knew the material they were teaching. I felt that my problem was the pain I was experiencing and everyone else in the group noticed I was in extreme pain and anguish, so they gave me permission to leave the program after a short time of being there in order to seek physical pain relief. At this time, I was also experiencing distorted thoughts; I felt that the program was put in place to teach me a lesson. I thought that everything that was occurring to me was influenced by someone with a lot of money who did not like me. I don't recall exactly what a patient told me, but I thought she was going to show up at my house three months latter to explain to me how everything that occurred there was a set up for a movie or simply to pull a prank on me. After I left the program, I waited and the girl did not show up, therefore I confirmed to myself that I was hallucinating.

My psychosis also affected other parts of my life negatively. I was asked to attend an interview to be accepted to a master's Program, but due to feeling unbalanced I did not attend the interview. If it had been before the (incident) concussion I would have been more than confident in myself that I would have answered all questions appropriately and been accepted. I felt that there was something wrong with my judgment and that I could not control how I responded to a question or event. I felt that if I were asked any type of question, I could burst like I did at my attorney's office, by burst I mean my emotions could get out of control. I felt that I was in no control of my emotions or judgment. My concussion hindered my intellect, and stability.

I felt that nothing in my life was going right. I was in a rut and there was nothing I could do about it. I had heard stories of people doing witch craft on other people and I had discovered that a close friend of mine believed in WICA, which I believed might have done witch craft on me; therefore, I believed someone did witch craft on me, so I decided to try to find out if someone had done it to me and do something about it.

I was extremely desperate and willing to try anything in order for my life, health and overall situation to get better, which led me to investigate by going to a lady who was highly referred to me from Los Angeles who knew how to read tarot cards. I went to her and asked her if she could read my tarot cards and she told me during the reading that she did not see in the cards that someone had done a witch craft on me, but she did see that I was stuck and going in circles. I agreed with her tarot reading, but the frustration in my voice of things having gone wrong for such a long time perhaps made her want to look further to check if indeed it was true because she stated that perhaps someone had done witch craft on me, but it was a hidden job. I decided to pay her to find out, since it was a reasonable price of $600, which I could afford. I left her office and in a short time I saw Mark. I did not know it was Mark at the time.

It was not until more than a year later after studying the bible with a Jehovah witness and confessing myself with a Catholic priest that I discovered who it was. I discovered it was Mark 28:14. I was becoming closer to God by studying the bible when I realized that what I saw was Mark. Mark looked like Sméagol from the Lord of the Rings. He was an elderly man who looked like he was carrying a baby in his arms, but in the bible, he is described as an elderly man carrying a mantle in his arms. When I saw Mark, I was very scared, and I did not know what to do. I simply thought that the lady who was going to check if someone did a hidden job to hurt me had checked.

I soon went to the lady who read tarot cards after the incident to see what her findings were. She read my tarot cards once again and told me that my luck was still bad and she told me that she saw two men whom were doing something bad to me and that one day I would find out whom these two men were. In my mind I could never believe that a man would try to hurt me, I thought perhaps it was a woman because of my friend who believed in witchcraft, but the lady insisted it was a man. More time passed and I was beginning to hear things around the month of October. I began to hear knocking noises on the wall, and I would get up from bed and stand in a thorn. I told a friend I would get up and stand in a thorn, but they told me it was probably from my garden and that the noises I was hearing in the wall was most likely rats. I believed them, but I was still scared and felt that I desperately needed to find God's forgiveness for seeing Mark and everything else in my life. This was one of the leading events in my life along with a few others, which got me to go confess myself one night of the anniversary of my baptism. I also had Mormons knock at my door, which was one of the many ways God was calling me to become closer with him. I felt that God was working through several religions to get closer to me.

Where there is life there is hope for many things. When there is life there is a chance to change; to find hope, to find salvation, to find the right path, to help others, to gain knowledge and wisdom of the things to come and are about to come. When I have lost hope of a better tomorrow the words "where there is life there is hope" has given me hope to make positive changes in my life. When all seems to fail, I have found that looking at my true DAD has picked me up from rock bottom, a point that I am disappointed to say I have reached in my life. We reach rock bottom when we least expect it and we think that it could never happen to us, but it can happen to anyone. When we least expect we can reach rock bottom but, the words that have lifted me up are "it could have been worse." It could have been worse shows us that even though we may not have everything that we want and desire it certainly can be worse. Therefore, we need to set a quiet time to thank our True DAD for the little things that make our day shine. It can be anything and it can be the simplest thing, but our appreciation to our True DAD will make things get better.

I reached rock bottom after being in a motor vehicle accident, which caused me to obtain post concussive syndrome, which if you did not know use to be called punched drunk syndrome and with a syndrome like this it is virtually impossible to make good choices and decisions. I made a lot of bad choices, which I regret and have come to my True DAD for forgiveness. I had a syndrome, which caused me to make bad choices in life and yet I never sat and contemplated that my choices were taking me straight to hell. I did not start thinking about hell until I started working for a facility that housed teenage boys who have committed petty crimes. I did not know how to help these people. I finally found out that the solution to getting them to the right path was to teach them about God. I realized that I should teach them about God as I was driving to work and there was a fire on the freeway and all I could think of was these boys are going to hell. I soon began to try to fix their problem while neglecting the fact that I too could be going to hell. I started teaching them about our True Dad and I realized that I was teaching them something that I was not even doing myself. I then realized that sometimes we need to think about ourselves first and then others because how can we expect others to do the things that we do not do ourselves. Do what I say and not what I do seemed a little hypocritical.

There are times in our lives when we need to analyze our situation and do what we expect others to do. I soon realized that I could not help another person until I found help myself from self-destruction because that was exactly where I was heading in life and I did not even know it. I had reached a point where I was recovering from having post concussive syndrome, but I was still living a self-destructive lifestyle. I tried teaching the teenage boys about religion by showing them a video a friend of mine gave me who had been in prison for the same behavior the teenage boys were demonstrating. When in prison he found God and this video about God changed his life, so I tried showing it to the teenage boys when all of a sudden I realized I needed to take the spec out of my eye before I could take it out of somebody else's eye. The video was about a priest who tells his story of his troubled youth and how he ends up becoming a priest. It is a good story, and a part of a chain reaction of things, which happened to me, which brought me closer to God. A list of things happened to me in my life that has brought me closer to my DAD.

Everything in my life was stating that I needed God in my life including an astrology chart I got for my birthday to check if things were going to get better. The chart stated that I was going to become a deeply religious person. Everything in my life was pointing me to the desire that I needed God in my life to fortify me. I looked everywhere for answers to different types of doctors, astrology, different church congregations. My heart was desperate for a solution and I was not thinking straight. In some ways I felt like I had given up on myself. I am a sinner. After I was diagnosed with Post-concussion syndrome and had ADD symptoms, I began to give up on life. I was in a lot of pain and unable to focus and concentrate, due to some nerve damage, which caused me to do something I would have never thought of doing before. I tried methamphetamines about a dozen times. I do not do any types of drugs now that I have found God and am healthier, so to speak, but after my concussion it is sad to say that I had given up on life and in many ways wanted to die and could not believe that people would bring children in to this world if there could be so much pain.

My curiosity for illegal drugs began as I was being given Strattera by my psychologist in order to alleviate the symptoms; not knowing what the dose was for me, as well as my financial situation the doctor gave me sample bottles of different milligrams. I began to take different milligrams of Strattera, but when I got to 40 mg of Strattera, I can recall thinking that I could feel something different in my brain. I felt for a little while that I was normal, and I got down on my knees sobbing and pleaded to God to heal me. It was as if the medication helped me believe in God again. The medication did not work for me because soon after I was done with the 40mg sample I started taking 80 mg and the medication was making me feel upset or on edge. I felt like I had no hope and decided to try a drug that I had never thought I would try, since my logic was that the doctors were prescribing me methamphetamines so might as well try street drugs of meth, I was a disaster. I do not condone drugs unless you are sick and they are prescribed by a doctor, but I want you to know the truth of what I did. I had no energy or motivation because the pain I was feeling was draining me, but when I tried meth it awakened something in my brain and it helped my brain a lot. I felt like the meth was cleansing my brain. I was a different person when I was on meth. When I was on meth, I felt I was a kid again. I felt that meth helped me remember a more accurate traumatizing event, which had occurred with an attorney I had, as well as good memories I have had throughout my life. I remembered most of the things that happened to me at an attorney's office and could not stop talking about it to one of my close friends. I remembered most of the things that happened to me at the attorney's office, but it was not until I felt the Holy Spirit that I could put all the pieces of the puzzle of my life together.

On another occasion, I tried meth and when I went home, I started hallucinating. Meth felt like what others describe ayahuasca, a spiritual ceremony with an herb does to people to seek spiritual healing. I was doing my homework and as I was doing my homework, I began to quote the bible to prove a point I was writing about. I began to get feelings I had when I studied the Bible when I was eighteen years old and then proceeded to go to my mother's room and asked her to study the Christian Bible with me. My mother got scared of me, since I had wakened her up from her sleep to try to study the Bible with her. My mother got up and walked to the kitchen and seeing my determination and manic behavior she called the police. It did not take the police officer long to get to my house, since the police station is only a few minutes away. When the police officer came to my house I was determined to try to study the Bible with the police officer because the meth made my deeper feelings come out and I had begun to think that if I did not convert someone I was going to go to hell, since the bible teaches to be a disciple. The police officer did not want to study the bible with me, and I became terribly upset and ended up throwing a small coffee pot on the ground and broke it in several pieces. The police officer trying to calm me down asked me if I took any medications and I told him I did, but that I had forgotten to take it. He asked me were the medication was and I told him it was in my bedroom closet, but I was too scared to open my closet and get my medication, so he did it for me. He brought me my medication, which is called Nortriptyline, which is for migraines, which was given by a neurologist. I took it, but my symptoms did not get better. The police officer hand cuffed me and put me in the back seat of his vehicle. The entire night I was sending messages to all of my friends, due to my manic behavior and when I was in the police car one of my friends showed up and was terrified to see me in the back of the police car yelling and screaming. My friend began to cry to see me in such a situation. I started yelling to her to go to church and to stop sleeping with men. The police officer soon drove off to take me to the police station, but when I was at the police station, I was yelling for God to save me. This was not the last time I tried meth, I tried meth again a week before I decided to learn God's name.

When I was on meth my thoughts for God were intensified and I realized I was nothing without God. I desperately needed salvation, so one day I went to a priest in order to learn God's name and receive his salvation because I was told that God's name is our salvation by someone I was studying the Bible with. It was not until one day after confessing myself for the first time to a priest and felt the wholly spirit that all my pain went away. Fear the Lord and love him with all your heart and soul and accept that not everyone will go to Heaven; that is simply the law of nature and there is nothing one can do about it. I believe the only thing that a person can do for more to enter God's Kingdom is to pray for two Heavens.

After the accident I had a lot of emotional issues and physical pain. Some of my physical symptoms were my front abdominopelvic region was strained in the right lumbar regional, umbilical region and left lumbar region, tension and pain was developed in skull, cervical, thoracic, and lumbar regions of my axial skeleton. The right hemisphere of my head endured extreme tension, along with the rest of my head. An extreme discomfort and pain, especially while turning head, with extension and flexion of the neck. My headache- is the muscle tension type, with sharp, dull, and intense pain extending from the frontal lobe of the head to the occipital part of my skull. The headache, neck pain and stiffness were recurrent. The pain radiates to the shoulders and arms. There is an intermittent numbness of the arms and back of the head. The occipital part of my brain felt empty, as if there is a void or loss of chemical production due to the bruising to the brain. I endured emotional pain; past traumas arose, physical pain on all my body. The most enduring pain is head, neck, and back pain, as well as extreme tiredness developed. I developed an Anxiety neurosis, due to the pain, and imbalance in my head. I developed insomnia, due to the pain and swelling in my lower and upper back, as well as from the pain and imbalance in my head. I suffered from bilateral cervical spine pain, with extreme discomfort, which has disappeared after establishing contact with God, shoulder depression in my cervical right spine. I also suffered from *cervical spine range of motion lateral flexion* with pain, *decreased flexion*: with pain normal extension. Palpation: *Bilateral cervical spine- right cervical paraspinal muscles* and *levator, scapula* tenderness with identifiable trigger points, along with *muscle spasm—moderate with tenderness and identifiable trigger points. Cervical sprain/strain* and spasms, especially on the right side. *Cervical musculoligamentous* sprain and strain. A *bilateral cervical paraspinal* tenderness to palpation. Tenderness in the *upper trapezius* and *medial scapular ridge. Deep tendon reflexes in the snout, glabellar, palmomental and grasp reflexes* were absent. Tenderness and pain in the lower back area and lower *lumbar paraspinal* muscles bilaterally. At C3 and C4 (cervical spine), there is a *1.7 mm broad based disc protrusion* that effects the *thecal sac.* There is a *bilateral neuroforaminal* narrowing causing *encroachment* on the C4 exiting nerve roots. At C4 and C5 (cervical spine), there is a *1.9 mm broad based disc protrusion* that abuts the *thecal sac.* At C6 and C7 (cervical spine), there was a *1.9 mm broad based disc protrusion* that abuts the *thecal sac.*

I saw several doctors and I would give them descriptions of my headaches as, migraines: cervical pain in the right region, lower lumbar pain and upon doing exercise, pain down my left leg. I also endure emotional pain because I do not feel as capable with my intellectual abilities as I once did. I got irritated easily, and found it difficult to focus, due to head, neck, lower back, and side of left leg pain. I was very impulsive, due to the inability to focus or concentrate due to the anxiety that my cervical pain and head tension gave me putting me on edge.

The frequency and duration of my headaches varied, but I felt that they debilitated me in such a way that I did not find the energy to do anything. My energy levels varied throughout a day. My neck pain was the same way, at times my neck felt very stiff and tight or as hard as a rock, overall, my pain was constant. In the years that I was sick, I tried various treatments to get better. In one setting, I was placed in the seated position and made comfortable to be injected in the *right cervical paraspinal* trigger point and *right levator scapula* trigger point. A *25 gauge 1 ½ -inch needle* trigger point injections were sequentially performed in trigger points. A combination of *1 cc Kenalog 40 and, 4cc 2% Lidocaine and 4cc 0.25%.* Marcaine was evenly distributed into all trigger points. Superficial needling performed subsequently with twitch responses noted. For many years I took muscle relaxants: applied ice or heat, did exercises, and applied pain-relieving cream or spray on my back, neck and head not necessarily prescribed from the same doctor. I also used a posture pump to relieve pressure from my neck as much as possible. I took vitamins, such as L-tyrosine to focus, omega 3 for inflammation, gaba gamma-Aminobutyric Acid for my memory, Ashwagandha, Rhodiola extract and B-12 to increase my energy, which I obtained at GMC store. The vitamins helped me feel better when I would take them, but I could not always afford them. I got massages and used acupuncture on an as needed basis. I used a therapy bed almost every day to alleviate pain from building on my back to feel better. I had been bad for several years that I once even asked a doctor to pray for me before they treated me. I felt I needed God in my life. I did not take my medications for the first two years and spent most of my time in bed resting. When I started taking my medication again, I was able to go to work even though I was not perfectly better.

One day I wanted to know God's name. I felt I needed to know his name to be saved, therefore I went to church during the week at night, I took the bread, confessed my sins to a priest. I confessed for seeing an image of an old man and everything else in my conscience that was disturbing me. I love our creator a lot and because I love him a lot, I had the desire to want to learn more about him by studying with different Christian denominations. When I studied with different denominations I had a desire to want to know the truth and I learned that in learning Gods name we obtain salvation; therefore, I had a desire to want to get to know God more and to learn his name.

According to different documents God has different names, so I went to a church and took the Eucharistic and confessed myself. The person I confessed to blessed and told me to go and pray, when I prayed for God to tell me his name I felt a light come into me as the wholly spirit and I heard a voice the voice told me his Hebrew name and then he asked me if there was anything else I wanted to know. I told him that I also wanted to know if he was the one whom woke me up after a drowning accident and he said it was him. When I asked for his name, I was under so much desperation and I was scared because I had been going through an exceedingly difficult period in my life. I got up from praying and sat on a chair, but I began to tremble because I could not believe what had just happened to me. I was in shock and I thought something bad might happen to me, but then a group of people whom were worshiping came up to me and brought me to the front of the room and they put a blanket on top of me and began to pray over me. I soon felt a peace and happiness that took me out of the depression and desperation, which had first brought me to church in the first place. I walked out of church and the members of the church asked me what God had told me, since they saw a light and a peace enter the room, with great joy in my heart and peace in my soul I told the member that asked me that God had revealed his name to me. I left the church to return to my home and when I arrived home I told my mother that God had just revealed his name to me and then I went to my room and proceeded to text different people Gods name.

I spoke to my sister that night of November 21 and she did not believe me. She thought I was on drugs and should be put in a mental health institution for doing drugs. I then spoke to a friend of mine from a country called Bagdad and he told me that I was greedy and that I should put money underneath my pillow and give it to the first person I see in the morning. He told me that if I did not put the money underneath my pillow something bad would happen to me and I became scared. Therefore, I went to the bank and pulled out some money. I did not know how much money to put underneath the pillow, but having been talking to psychiatrist they got me to start thinking that everything in our lives relates to something else in our lives so I began to think that the amount of money that I put underneath my pillow could also represent the amount of years I was going to live and I did not want to be greedy, so I decided to put 40 dollars underneath my pillow thinking that that would be a good amount of time to live, since I did not want to experience the painful parts of life at old age. I thought it could get worse than the pain I was experiencing at the time. I was scared because I knew that I had done something bad in God's eyes.

I had not eaten in three days and I had been under the influence of meth because for a few times I had self-medicated myself from the symptoms of post concussive syndrome with meth. The meth was helping me focus on school because I had been diagnosed with post concussive syndrome after an auto accident and it was like having ADHD symptoms along with anxiety. I had awakened God and I was scared that something bad was going to happen to me, so I decided to listen to my friend from the country of Bagdad. That night I put money underneath my pillow and the entire night I was having a dream that I was asking God for forgiveness for all the sins that I had committed. All I kept saying over and over was that I was sorry, and I could see God in my dream, he looked like an invisible spirit. When I woke up in the morning, I was looking for my keys, but I could not find them, so I decided to walk outside and give the money to the first person I saw. I saw my next door neighbor whom I am not very acquainted with, but he did not want to take the money and then I looked to my right and saw a gardener cutting the branches from the trees I went up to him and asked him if he believed in God. He told me that he did and then I asked him what church he went to and it just so happen that he went to the church that was close to my house that I had gone to and felt the wholly spirit. I then proceeded to ask him if he could do me a favor by going to the church and giving a piece of paper with God's name to the preachers of the church. He agreed and I never saw the man again. For the next couple of days, I kept praying for people to believe me that I had felt God's presence and that what was happening to me was real and not a hallucination.

My mother then told me that she believed me and that she believed I had heard God's name. The economy had been bad and since I was diagnosed with post concussive syndrome, which is when your brain hits your skull and your brain swells giving you a lot of side effects such as depression and anxiety. I was not working; due to the concussion I had and therefore lost my home. I did not have any were to live so I went to live with my friend for a short time until I finished the semester in school because I was working towards obtaining a Master's degree in Marriage Family Therapy. I did not obtain that desired degree because right before I finished the semester, I felt the Holy Spirit again.

I was at work walking around a home depot. I was working as a vendor to get customers to reface their kitchen cabinets. I asked every customer in the store if they would like to reface there kitchen cabinets and all I kept getting from people was "No." I began to pray to God for him to help me with a lead, since I could not do it on my own, but that night I gave up early and decided to leave. I got in my car and drove off when suddenly, all the traffic stops, and a car hits me from behind. I begin to pray out loud and my voice sounds like I am singing as I call on God to help me and to forgive me for anything that I have done wrong. Then suddenly, I hear a voice and it is God talking to me, he tells me that he is with me. I get scared because I begin to think that God is with me and I get hit by a car I must be in big trouble. The guy that is driving the car behind me jumps out of his car and runs to hide somewhere. The woman in the passenger side comes out of the car and walks towards my passenger side window and asks me what I said. I told her I said God's name and she said her husband heard me say it and got scared and that was the reason why he ran out of the car. I called the cops to do a police report and they could not find the women's husband that hit me. I did not want to make a big deal, so I told the cop that I was okay and that I did not need to go to the emergency room, so I left. I went to my friend's house and she decided to take me to the emergency room any way based on my previous history of being hit by a car and getting post concussive syndrome. I went to the emergency room and nothing was wrong with me, I was relived.

Later that week I had a presentation to do for my group therapy class. My presentation is on how to seek a higher power. I ask my classmates what their higher power is, and everyone has a different answer. I hear God talk to me and he tells me to tell them his name, but then I was interrupted by a girl whom wanted me to finish fast so I did not get to tell the class God's name or the experience that had recently occurred to me. I handed in my presentation to my teacher and sat in my seat. I was very shocked and do not understand what is going on with me. I am done with my semester and the next semester starts because I was going to adult school and every semester is like a month to three months long. I decide not to register for another semester until I figure out what is going on with me and move out of my friend's house.

I decide to move to Mexico where I have a family member live, since I had recently lost my home. When I moved to Mexico I began to hear God talk to me more, at first I was surprised and was not sure if it was God, but I remember him giving me his name and knew it was him as I began to read the bible from beginning to end and the bible stories I read matched with his character traits and actions. I learned a lot about God through the conversations he would have with me. I learned that all roles and titles are given to our Lord and that he knows more than we think. He knows everything. He knows all the laws. He knows every man, women, and child by name. He knows what was in the beginning, middle and has seen almost everything. He invented science and all that is divine. He knows what we think and what is in our core; and has created every person differently. He told me that no two people in this world think alike. He created the Heavens and the Earth and everything in between.

When God spoke to me, He spoke to me about everyday things. He talked to me about His character and that He is invisible. We talked about my dog and how my dog would like me to heat up his food in the microwave to things that were too difficult for me to comprehend because God is a very complex being and some of the things he would tell me were mind blowing, and I told him I was not prepared to know the secrets to the universe so he stopped telling me how he determines and comes up with decisions, in other words I could not believe I was speaking to God. God told me that in the beginning he was all alone for a long time, until one day he made his children. Before he made his children, he searched everywhere to see if there was another God like himself and he did not find one.

While he spoke to me he looked again to make sure if there was another God like him and still after all of this time that has passed, there's still no other God like him and he is still looking because he has not meet his match yet, and at the same time, he does not want anybody else to be like him and to have the same powers that he has.

It is not a small world after all, so it took God a while to search everywhere to see if there was another God. So, after his search, it turns out there is only one God in the whole entire Universe and there is no other God like him. We spoke about various topics. We also spoke about my biological male parent. He told me that there was something about me that he liked and that he liked my family background. He liked that my biological male parent had a lot of children and that at first, he was jealous and mad. He is no longer mad that my male parent had a lot of children, and said he got over the fact that a lot of people called him Dad.

My biological Dad was Dr. Benji and he was an only child for long time. He always wanted to come from a big family, so he decided to have a lot of children. He had more than 28 children and he planned to have them. He named all his children and was a particularly good father because he was in every one of his children's life as much as possible. He was a highly active man who was told that he was going to die at the age of 13 due to heart problems but ended up living a long full life. He became a Neurosurgeon and worked for the CIA. He died in an auto accident on a very unlucky day Friday, September 13 on the 405 FRWY from a heart attack. He was a tall man with curly hair and could grow a full beard. He made precise cuts with his hands when he performed surgeries and loved to travel. When I was a little girl I drowned and was resurrected, when I resurrected, I saw both my dad's on the same day. I saw God and he told me I would see him again and then I woke up and saw my biological dad. I was always worried for my biological dad's soul since he died on a very unlucky day, but one day God let me talk to my biological Dad in Heaven and he told me that he did not like the day that he died either and that he had already lived his life and it was time for me to live mine. I thought it was incredibly good advice and I was grateful to God for letting me talk to him. When I spoke to God, I learned how important it is for God to be called Dad. He wants everyone to call him Dad when we see him in Heaven, and he wants us to ask him for living water because in Heaven they drink a lot of water and water is especially important. God is our Dad and the word Dad is like music to Gods ears. He likes to be called God and Jehovah, but Dad is by far the greatest name we can call him. I later learned that the reason I had had so many bad things happen to me was because I had been greedy by praying for everyone to go to Heaven. I prayed for everyone to go to Heaven and when someone prays for everyone to go to Heaven bad things will a happen to the person. So many bad things happened to me, such as being in a lot of pain and having post concussive syndrome and anxiety. I was lucky that I did not have the heart of an animal, but I felt that I had given up on life and that nothing mattered or was important.

When I had post concussive syndrome there were many days that I could not believe what was happening to me and I even felt like dying. There were times when I would get down on my knees and cry out to God why this was happening to me and I was grateful as I felt the medication I was taking at the time made me believe in God and helped me cry out to God and took me out of the glazed state I was in the first two years of my concussion. I wanted God in my life so bad that I asked him to help me with all of my heart and soul and God liked the way I asked him so one day when I needed to know his name after taking the Eucharistic at a local church and the priest told me to go pray God revealed his name to me and later told me to call him DAD and that the reason he picked me had to do with my biological Father because he had a lot of children.

Today our Father has forgiven me and asked me to ask people to pray for me. I feel that knowing our True Father has improved my life so I want to teach you what I know so that your life may also be filled with his blessings. Every person needs to work towards their own salvation; there is no prayer that will save our entire humanity. Every person needs to work towards their own salvation by doing good deeds, being a good person and most importantly loving our Dad. I have learned by speaking to God that nobody knows who is going to enter Gods Kingdom because it can be anybody only God knows who is going to enter his kingdom and that a lot of people go to Heaven because a lot of people are good in Gods eyes. People go to Heaven by taking a first step of baptism and God wants everyone to get baptized even if they think they are not going to Heaven and if we think we are not going to Heaven he still wants us to try. He wants everyone to get baptized, it does not matter if you are not a virgin and have been per miscues or feel you are a sinner, he wants you to repent and get baptized. He wants everyone to try to go to Heaven and spend time with him. Baptism is a marriage with God that helps initiate a relationship with God, it is acceptable to get baptized at any age, but 80 years old is too late in your life and he would prefer a person to get baptized early in life. Our creator adores us all; it does not matter if you are tall; short, fat, skinny, poor, or rich. He sees your heart and wants you to be devoted to him. He has a fondness for us that is magnanimous, it is enough for many. Your adoration will be reciprocated with his unconditional love.

When God spoke to me, he spoke to me in both a female and a male voice. He can change his voice to sound like anyone and anything. He has both sexes and created us in his image female and male. One time when he spoke to me, he barked at me like a dog because I assumed, he was mad at me. Another incident in which he became upset with me was when I had gone to a local church in Mexico and asked were in the Bible did it say that the Virgin Mary rose whole into Heaven. I had asked this question at a Bible study because I had learned as a Christian that we should always quote the Bible to prove certain facts. I did not believe that what I did was wrong; but that night when I went home, and I was sleeping in my bed I was suddenly awakened. I felt a hand grab me from the front of my shirt and I could see the outline of the hand folded in a semi invisible matter. I should have been terrified because I was flouting on top of my bed as I looked to my side and noticed that I was off my bed and up in the air. I was in dismay and did not know what was going on, but suddenly, I hear a voice tell me I have always wanted to do this. I thought to myself why and then I realized that he was lifting me because I had asked were in the Bible does it say that the Virgin Mary rose whole. God then spoke to me and told me that he knew I liked him a lot' and therefore put me down. I knew he was mad at me by the way his faced looked, but he did not do anything terrible to me he simply put me back down on my bed. I felt a peace that I had never felt before, it was like his presence had a mechanism of love, warmth and peace that I had always desired and even though he was mad at me I was not scarred. He turned around and walked out my window and I was in disbelief about what had just happened to me. I stared blankly in front of me and then he gave me something to go to sleep because I fell asleep right away.

There were some instances that he would talk to me when I was sleeping. He would show me when I was sleeping that he could hear my thoughts and that he could go right threw me. I could see him standing right beside my bed. Sometimes he looked like a black shadow and other times he looked like a cartoon with the same light blue outer color that fire has so that I could see him in the dark, he was a shape shifter. One time he even looked as a dog as he barked at me. I was terrified about what he could do, but I had peace in my heart because I said to myself, he means no harm to me. He was showing me what he could do, and I was mesmerized.

In our conversations God told me to be good, so I decided to stay single. He told me to tell people to get married and have children. God likes it when people are faithful and monogamous, so try not to be per miscues because God is our Father and he will like us better if we are abstinent or monogamous, but you are allowed to sleep with whomever you want because you have free will, but he does not like that.

Be a leader, be unique, be different, try to stand out above the rest, be yourself and most importantly forgive others in the same way that you would like to be forgiven by God. Also do your best to follow the laws of the Nation and always put God first in your life. Pray that our laws are up to Gods standards and pray for the positive desires of your heart.

When he was speaking to me there was a couple of incidents when he told me he was searching the world to see if there was another God and that he found that the Universe is enclosed by walls and God cannot go through them. The concept of the Universe being enclosed by walls brought to my attention Cindy's Religious Philosophical Question: The question in philosophy is if God is real, but in religious philosophy the belief is that God is real, but is there another God in another Universe, which neither our God or any human know about ?What If? I thought to myself. God has a real great sense of humor and the reason he told me that he was searching the world had to do with a document I was reading regarding God and the Universe.

When I told people, I heard god's voice they thought I had a mental illness and God told me that was how Moses felt when he was alive. God has very short conversations with me, but one thing I tell you is that God is real and I advocate for everyone to love him with all of their heart, as much as possible for he is our Dad. Loving God is like flirting with death for he is the one we find on the other side of our human life. Love everything that has to do with God and most importantly love people of God and quote them and teach others about God as well as think positive thoughts.

I prayed for everyone to go to Heaven and that very same day I took it back, but God said that when I prayed for everyone to go to Heaven I meant it so he punished me for it, if I had not taken it back perhaps my punishment would have been a lot worse. My punishment consisted of me wishing I were dead and having the mind of beast. I am living out the rest of my days loving God for he is my Father.

God tired of talking to me and for a while I did not go back to work or to school. I was diagnosed with schizophrenia and decided to spend most of my days at church, but eventually decided not to go to church for the people, but for God so even though I knew I should be a part of the body of Christ I decided to use my body as a temple to worship my Dad mostly from home or out in nature. I spent most of my days loving one direction, which is heaven, being single and living with my older sister until I ventured out to live alone. God told me that he thought I was easy and therefore he was not pleased with me, but with time he forgave me and gave me one of the names to enter his kingdom YAVES, which is one of his names in the Spanish bible. He told me I would live the rest of my days being poor, but he was good with me because I was thankful for every little thing that I had. My physical symptoms eventually went away, and I was mostly in better health. I took vitamins from GMC for brain function and they helped me focus and have energy.

When I was in my Dads presence I felt a peace that I had never felt before, it was like his presence had a mechanism of love, warmth and peace that I had always desired and even though he was mad at me I was not scarred. He turned around and walked out my window and I was in disbelief about what had just happened to me. I stared blankly in front of me and then he gave me something to go to sleep because I fell asleep right away. There were some instances that he would talk to me when I was sleeping. He would show me when I was sleeping that he could hear my thoughts and that he could go right threw me. I could see him standing right beside my bed. Sometimes he looked like a black shadow and other times he looked like a cartoon with the same light blue outer color that fire has so that I could see him in the dark, he was a shape shifter. One time he even looked as a dog as he barked at me. I was terrified about what he could do, but I had peace in my heart because he meant me no harm, I told myself. He was showing me what he could do, and I was mesmerized.

My message to the world…

I made a huge mistake of praying for everyone to go to Heaven and I severely payed for it and I do not want the story to repeat itself even though I already know that the story will most likely repeat itself because the wholly spirit told me so. Whatever you do in this world do not let the words "only a few shall enter Gods Kingdom "scare you into praying for more to enter his kingdom because God knows before anyone is born whom will enter and whom will not enter his kingdom so please do not waste your time praying for everyone to enter Gods Kingdom because if you do you will go to hell and back and you will regret it with all of your being as I have. We only live once, so enjoy your life and only a very, very few will enter Gods Kingdom, but whatever you do love God with all of your heart and never stop praying for that is our purpose in life. In any case if you do not want to lose hope pray for two Heavens so that more people can enter his Kingdom. I was not able to enter Gods Kingdom when I was three years old after a drowning accident and will never be accepted by everyone in Heaven. Pray for God to always have mercy and love towards me so that I do not have to live life like a caged bird. Pray for one another and live a happy life and be fun. I am becoming the person God wants me to be and I am where I am because we are where God wants us to be in life. Our Dad will help us, but we must also learn to help ourselves and to open our hearts to have him help us.

The Lion and the King…

In India, there is a story of a King who is told that he is going to be eaten by a lion. The King gets scared because he does not want to get eaten by the lion that symbolizes the devil, but he is told that if he hurts himself he will not get eaten by a lion, which is a symbol of going to hell; therefore the King cuts himself when he is told that the lion will not eat him if he is injured and therefore, the lion does not eat him and he does not go to hell. The King becomes saved through an injury he has placed on himself to not be eaten by the lion and does not go to hell. The lion represents the devil in the story and how the devil does not obtain those that are injured because those that are injured have a chance to seek our Dad.

This story of the King in India has a major significant to a similar situation that happened to me. I was injured and, due to this injury I got closer to God and through becoming knowledgeable of his true name obtained salvation and therefore I have created this document to help others seek a higher power, especially in times of distress. Please share this document with the sick, anguished and those with anxiety, stress, and difficulty to help them understand that things will get better with God on their side and with a lot of prayer. We are currently living in a time of distress and I know this document will help people seek our Dad. Give this document to the sick outside of hospitals, to your neighbors, friends, loved ones and even enemy because we want to forgive others in the same way that we would like to be forgiven. This document will help many people become one with our Dad.

I have been lucky enough to have signs given to me by our Dad, since I was very young and I want my experiences to help others seek our Dad more and to love him more and to go towards him and ask him to live within you.

A Sign…

When I was in my teens I asked for a sign from above and to my dismay it was given to me. I had reached a time in my life where I wanted to begin to date and I wanted a sign from above to tell me if I should begin to date and as a couple of friends came over for a barbeque I asked God for a sign and as I asked this question the frames on the walls fell down and so did the boom boxes in my living room. My couple of friends who came over for the barbeque became frightened and so did I. I was so amazed at the promptness of my sign that I told myself I would never ask for a sign again.

I have come to realize that even though our teens signify a time of leaving childhood behind and entering adulthood it is our Fathers wishes to do our best to save our man and womanhood for our wedding night. It is especially important to our Father, for us not to be per miscues and to do our best to save ourselves for our wedding night. I did not do this, but through building a relationship with God I have come to know the importance of doing this. Throughout life I didn't always remember the sign I received in my living room, but in order to help all children of God be in better terms with our Dad I now share it with the ones I love in order for you to have a better relationship with God and for God to treat you better. Try to be monogamous and to genuinely love each other.

One day I will be gone, but for those who are living, I want to share the importance of marriage and faithfulness even though ultimately God gave us free will and he forgives everything but does not forget anything. So may the power of the wholly spirit help those who struggle with love find love in the right places. I learned that we should not ask for signs if we are not ready to hear a righteous answer and always try to do the right thing by looking into your heart and searching your thoughts by putting it down on paper and speaking to others in order to never have skeletons in your closet.

Fasting...

When our health is ill and our luck is down and everything we have tried seems to fail, fasting is the best way to try to be heard by God. When a person fast and prays, God has been known to hear us more and cure our illnesses. In my personal life I have fasted on several occasions, and the fasting method that worked best for me and I recommend for you is a concoction of different methods that have been used by others.

The first day that you start you may obtain a gallon of water and add sea salt, in about an hour you will need to use the restroom, your bowls will be empty but if you eat you will need to use the restroom right away. It is an organic way to cleanse your body, and then you may proceed to do the following to keep yourself from eating. You may do the following without having to use a sea salt as enamel. Try to fast on several occasions, and see which method works best for you if both together and or simply the lemonade juice by itself.

Obtain a container that can hold a gallon of liquid and fill the container ¾ of the way with water and then proceed to fill the container with the lemon juice from 12 lemons and then proceed to add maple syrup all the way to the top of the container. Obtain Grade D Maple Syrup that is organic; obtain cayenne pepper two tablespoons, obtain 6-(12) lemons that are organic depending on size (I have used nonorganic lemons, but it works best with organic lemons). Obtain a container to place the following ingredients in and carry with you to drink throughout the day when you get hungry and to keep your energy level high. The lemons, Cain pepper, and maple syrup should taste like a cola lemon aid, these ingredients have all the vitamins and nutrients that your body needs, especially if all the ingredients are organic. (Obtained from the Master Cleanser)

When you are done fasting you may eat whatever you want in moderation says the Lord. Try to eat healthy to have a long life and treat your body as the temple it is to praise our Dad.

FIFTH JOURNEY - GUIDANCE

Positive Affirmations

I am a positive, loving, energetic, funny, caring person who loves our creator and humanity.

I am glowing with health and wholeness with my creator on my side.

All the things I want, and need come to me with the help of my creator and others.

I always receive more than what I need from our creator and others.

I am successful with the help of our creator.

Everything I do turns into success with the help of our creator.

I attract positive-minded people into my life with the help of our creator.

I am attracting powerfully, positive, and healthy people into my life with the wholly spirit in my heart.

I draw all things positive to myself with the help of my creator.

I am a confident and positive person, and confident and positive persons gravitate to me with the help of our creator.

I am winning in all my relationships, with the help of our Dad.

I am caring, smart, supportive, loyal, and fun to be with and loved by our Dad.

I feel completely at ease and comfortable with all types of people and God.

I am a positive complete person who has the wholly spirit in my heart.

I behave in ways that promote my health and love for the wholly spirit every day.

I deserve to be in perfect health and our creator forgives me with his presence.

I can seek help from others and from the wholly spirit in times of need.

I let go of the past so I can walk in my Father's footsteps now.

I create health by expressing love, understanding, compassion and praise to the Lord.

I know that I deserve Love and accept it now from the universe.

I give out love and it is returned to me multiplied by the universe.

I rejoice in the love I encounter every day from others and our True Father.

Loving myself and others heals my life.

I choose to make positive healthy choices for myself and my salvation.

When I believe in myself so does God.

I express my needs and feelings and the wholly spirit hears me.

I am my own unique special-self, creative and wonderful and God loves me.

I am at peace when I am with God.

I trust in the process of life.

God is my True Dad and he loves me so.

Stay positive and when your mind wonders to the negative side listen to Gods positive words.

CHART to Success - GOD HAS A POSITIVE ANSWER

YOU SAY	Dad SAYS	We All Say
You say: 'It's impossible'	Dad says: **All things are possible**	With God everything is possible
You say: 'I'm too tired'	Dad says: **I will give you rest**	With God we will have rest
You say: 'Nobody really loves me'	Dad says: **I love you**	With God I feel loved
You say: 'I can't go on'	Dad says: **My grace is sufficient**	With God I can go on forever
You say: 'I can't figure things out'	Dad says: **I will direct your steps**	With God I will find my way
You say: 'I can't do it'	Dad says: **You can do all things**	With God everything is possible
You say: 'I'm not able'	Dad says: **I am able**	With God I am capable
You say: 'It's not worth it'	Dad says: **It will be worth it**	With God it will be worth it
You say: 'I can't forgive myself'	Dad says: **I Forgive you**	With God I will find forgiveness
You say: 'I can't manage'	Dad says: **I will supply all your needs**	With God all my needs will be meet
You say: 'I'm afraid'	Dad Says: **That is not what I say**	With God you will have no fear
You say: 'I'm always worried and frustrated'	Dad says: **Cast all your cares on ME**	With God I will have peace of mind
You say: 'I'm not smart enough'	Dad says: **I give you wisdom**	With God I will have wisdom

| You say: 'I feel all alone' | Dad says: I will never leave you or forsake you

May the Dad says become the You say on your journey to staying positive and walking with the Lord, so we can all stay positive with the Lord.

Let us Say: Stay positive in all of life circumstances and good things will happen because what we think influences God, so think positively. | With God I will never be alone |

Not Following God's Footsteps...

When people are not following our Dad's footsteps and are being selfish, greedy, boastful, and conceited; insulting, disobedient to their parents, ungrateful, and irreligious; unkind, merciless, slanders, *violent*, and fierce; hate the good; have treacherous behavior, are *reckless*, and swollen with pride; they will love pleasure rather than God; reject God and his real power. There will be negative consequences in society. One will see that there will be more members in society who have symptoms off ADD, anxiety and depression because they are lacking to put God first in their life. Put our Dad first and fight the evil in the world with kindness and love.

Life is Worth Living For - Fight...

Life is worth living for

Be a man who has everything

Give it what you can

It is worth the battle

Do not give up living free

Roar and claw your paws

Give it all you can

Fight like a mean tiger and bear

Soon it will be over

Use love as your tool to fight

WHO IS...?

I hope that you contemplate on the following **"Who is Questions."**

They have been designed to help you contemplate on what is your drive-in life. Contemplate on every question and be true to yourself. Everybody will have a different answer at the beginning, but I hope that as time passes your answers will be enlightened.

Who is Wonderful? Who is Awesome?

Who has every body's Bar Code?

Who is Kind? Who is great?

Who Has the Most Loving Heart?

Who is our Protector? Who is Divine?

Who Loves You? Who is Compassionate?

Who is Omnipotent? Who is in Control?

Who is the Cream Filling in your Apple Pie?

Who Is Forgiving? Who is on our minds all the time?

Who is the Fuel in your Engine?

Who is Amiable? Who is Amazing at Everything?

Who is the Light in your Lamp?

Who is perfect? Who Created the Universe?

Who is all? Who is our Timekeeper?

Who Is the Most Loving God?

Who Is Our Salvation?

Who is the Most Loving Father?

Who is the buckle in your belt?

Who has many roles in life?

Who is the Key to your Doorknob?

Who is Everything In this World?   Who can accomplish any task?

Who is the Dressing in your Salad?   Who is the Glue that Brings Us Together?

Who is the Ink in your Pen?   Who Knows Everybody's Name?

Who Is Your Inspiration?

I hope that you have evaluated the questions and thought long and hard on what your drive-in life is. My goal for you is to develop a relationship with God and to love God with all of our heart and soul and for you to answer most of these questions with God, Our True Father whom from now on we will refer to as "DAD." May his divine power complement your life. One step to making God the focus and healing component in your life is to get to know him; therefore, we will focus on getting to know him.

WHERE WERE YOU WHEN GOD CREATED THE UNIVERSE...?

After I finished writing my program for a counseling class and finished my class, I went to a counselor to speak about my problems because the universe was revealing itself to me. I was beginning to understand what was going on with me, but I did not know how to explain it to anyone. I did not know how to start the conversation with my therapist, but she made me feel comfortable because she was wearing a necklace with a cross around her neck. When I saw the cross around her neck, I was glad because I felt that she might just understand what was happening to me because I sure did not. I was simply going with the moment.

I explained to my counselor how I had just been hit by a car, but before this happened all the traffic had stopped and after I got hit by a car I started praying because I became very frightened. While I was praying, I heard the wholly spirit tell me that he was with me. I felt that if God is with me and I am being hit by a car then I must be in great trouble. I continued to pray out loud for God to help me and forgive me. Please forgive me came out of my mouth like a beautiful melody I have never heard myself sing. The driver from the car behind me got out of the driver's seat and ran. I continued to pray. My prayer sounded like a song. When I stopped praying, the wife of the driver came to me and asked me what I had just said. I told her I had said Gods name and she told me that her husband could hear what I was saying. He was afraid and ran out of the car and she did not know where he was hiding. He had run to her apartment, which was in front of the accident and told my counselor very quickly. I cannot remember exactly what I had told her during our session. I was rambling because I told her in short sentences that I had spoken to a priest, seen an old man in a dream and was uncertain of what was going on with me. I tried to explain to her that it was God, our DAD who had something to do with all the events that were happening in my life. I then questioned her and where were you when God created the universe. She became silent and somewhere I could sense that my questioning made her believe me because she became silent. I questioned her about the universe because that is what I felt God was doing to me. When I asked her about the universe, she believed that it was God's will for me to ask her that question. The tables had turned and instead of the therapist asking me questions I was asking her what I thought God was asking me and I think it helped me not sound crazy, but believable and that those unique experiences were in fact occurring to me, which I did not know how to unravel.

I did not know at the time, but I know now that God was in fact asking me this question because I had prayed for everyone to go to Heaven, it was as if God was telling me and who do you think you are to pray for such a thing, you do not know anything. I feel that God was challenging me because I do not know nothing about why things in society and the world are the way that they are. The universe is the way that it is for a reason and now my only solution is to pray for two Heavens for I have come to understand Gods plan a little more than most.

A related story, which I suggest you read, which got me to question were I was when the universe was created was Job 37:4-41... Am I crazy or is God really talking to me?

After I was hit by a car for the second time nothing happened to my car during the accident. I was afraid that I would be injured like I was in the first accident I was in a few years earlier, so I went to the emergency room, but everything was okay. I finished my last class after this incident and dropped out of school to live in Mexico. When I was in Mexico is when God started talking to me about all kinds of topics. When I came back to USA, he told me that I did something bad in his eyes and that I was always going to be poor and bored until further notice. He also told me that a lot of people go to Heaven because I was afraid that nobody went because I did not enter when I was a young child.

God's name is not Jehovah, but he likes to be called Jehovah. God does not want anyone to use his name in vein, so I did not reveal his real name. When I used his real name weird things happened in order for me to know that it was God answering my prayers and not a mere accident that what I asked for was coming true and sometimes it was a little scary because one could see just how powerful God truly is.

Jehovah is the cohesion to my life. He is my salvation, and I will sing to him. He is the glue that keeps me together and I will worship him, for he is my Dad and my Fathers Dad.

This is who I am, and this is whom I will always be. I am united with God.

LOONEY BIN...

I have not been to a looney bin in a long time, but previously I was in and out of the looney bin like it was no bodies business. I started hearing voices in November of 2010, at first the voices, which were coming from divine beings including God were nice to me, but then I did something wrong and they taught me that Gods plans are greater than our plans and his thoughts are greater than my thoughts. His thoughts were too great for me. The voices I hear control me because they tell me to stay single and not to get married and I listen to them because I know it is a higher power talking to me. They told me to tell others to get married and have children. They diagnosed me with schizophrenic effective disorder because I also see images of divine beings and depression because my energy is down. My life was a lot different than it was before the accident because I did not work for a long time and my finances were low.

How I Kept Myself Occupied...

I kept to myself and occupied myself by doing daily tasks like walking the dog, Facebooking, painting, going to the gym, and watching movies. I watched movies like Friends on Netflix. One of my favorite characters is Febbie, I like the fact that she turned out to be a happy person although her mother killed herself. I hope my nieces and nephew turn out as positive as Febbie because they have gone through a similar situation as Febbie. There dad was in jail as the number one suspect of killing their mother, which the wholly spirit told me he was innocent of. He has been released from jail after serving 6 years as it was a hung jury, and he was given a plea bargain. I know she killed herself. It is a tragic story.

Sometimes all you can do is have faith and hope for the best, meditate, pray, think positively, and believe in a higher power.

I had low energy levels therefore I didn't work for a long time and I didn't have much money, but I want to give love to the world, how do I give to the community, I soon started working in the Human Services Field where I was able to make a positive difference with people in the community who have experienced mental health issues.

We are currently going through a difficult time in the world, and we are living in the last days. National pandemics have taken place and we have practiced social distancing to prevent from becoming ill, but I know that with prayer all these things will get better. The world is currently overpopulated, and things will be in balance with prayer. I hope that we practice social distancing and spend more times with our families when pandemics occur in history. I hope we are teaching the young generations values, morals, good conduct, and how to be law abiding citizens in their young adult lives, as well as adulthood. Love yourself; feed yourself nutritious foods, exercise, smile at neighbors and friends because even when wearing a mask your eyes also give out a glimmer of a smile. When social distancing is over: be who you are, give tighter hugs and keep a clean home. Pick a day out of the week to clean the bathrooms and vacuum because as they say cleanliness is next to Godliness. Let us stay connected to our loved ones, wash your hands, take showers, use soap when washing your clothes, help your neighbor, friend, and family members. Let us appreciate the things we take for granted and try to always be thankful to our creator and True Father. Life may not always go as planned, but eventually it will turn out the way God plans. Sometimes we need to be alone not to be lonely, but to enjoy free time with yourself.

Woman…

There are many types of woman. An easy woman not pleasing in Gods eyes. A strong woman seeking God's forgiveness. A brave woman fears the Lord her Father. A courageous woman stands up for what she believes in. All woman united are untouchable Woman are the next generation changing their roles with time and receiving God's blessing. Woman come in all shapes, sizes, color and are loved by God. A woman can be a deacon, teacher, doctor or saint and sinful woman go to heaven too.

Beauty…

A beauty that is sweet and tender Soft and delightful like a red, orange rose on a summer's day. Smells of sweet nectar and captivates the sight. Long stem, fragile and yet strong with thorns that pierce. A beauty that is charming.

A Day in My Life…haiku

On a spring day walking the brown dog outside. Sun shining on face Sun high in the sky Pool turning into a green swamp. Cannot take a dive. Handyman out of sight. The circuit breaker is broken. Anticipating jump. A warm sunny day. Waiting for green to turn blue. Exploring options.

A Mother's Love...

A mother's love. You saw me grow and as I grew you saw me sprout into a woman. Your love seemed so strict, but I knew you only wanted to keep me safe. Now I am so glad you were strict because I see things more clearly now.

Your love was there when I had trouble with boys, or when I was simply feeling under the weather. Your love was there during all the technical difficulties in my life. There is no love like the love of a mother who is always there when you fall by helping you get back up. You dreamed big for all your children. Mother you are the best simply one of a kind. A good woman has a big heart; she is a good listener, cares about the well-being of others and can help pick you up when you are down. A good woman is like a treasure of ruby and diamonds. She does not cheat or steal unless it is your heart she is stealing. Do not take a good woman for granted because if you do someone else will appreciate what you did not.

A good woman follows our True Fathers word. A good woman tries to keep her children safe, well nourished, clothed, bathed, housed, and has faith in the Lord that he will help her provide those things and more.

A Good Man Statement...

A good man will be there for his family and children. He will be a loving, nourishing person. He will also follow our True Fathers word. He will not take a good woman for granted because if he does someone else will appreciate what he did not. A good man will love our Dad above all things and appreciate all that life has to offer.

CONCLUSION

Lord you are my courage, strength, rock, pillar, and I pray for better days.

Share this book with the sick at hospitals, share with the healthy, give to a friend or loved one. Quote and read it and may the belief in our True Father become stronger than it has ever been throughout our towns, cities, counties, states, countries, and world. He is real and can do all things through prayer. Lord we love you for you are our Father and most powerful DAD.

When we are injured or feeling broken there is a chance for redemption and forgiveness and a chance to be amongst the angels in Heaven. The devil will not be able to take you for we are reminded that we are our True Fathers children, as well as that the Lord is all powerful and merciful. Have faith and never give up on believing.

I was also told as a small child to not be afraid after I was accidently burned by tar that fell off the roof of my home, while contractors were fixing the roof. I believe that the tar being hot was a simile to fire and in my mind I always believed to not be afraid of the devil because that is what my biological dad told me as a small child and now as I reflect I know I am right for we should only fear the Lord our True Father for to fear the Lord is wise, even though some may argue why should we fear the Lord when God is love and yes our True Father is love, peace and happiness, but the world is so complex at times that having fear to Our True Father means having wisdom because he is so complex, wise, shrewd and all-knowing and his love for us is so great, it is magnanimous that if a King were injured he would not allow a lion, which is a symbol for the devil to take the king, but instead up lift the King so it can fly like a butterfly. Fear is a form of respect I have for my True Father.

To be continued for tomorrow is an unknown journey.

REFERENCES:

Holy Bible, New King James Version, Review and Herald Publishing Associates, 1990

La Biblia Latina Americana, San Pablo / Editorial Verbo Divino; 65a edicion edition (2005) (Latin American Spanish Bible)

Lightning Source UK Ltd.
Milton Keynes UK
UKHW020802101120
373087UK00002B/136